Joanna Murray-Smith's plays have been produced throughout Australia and all over the world. They include *Honour*, *The Female of the Species*, *Songs for Nobodies*, *Rockabye*, *Ninety*, *Bombshells*, *Rapture*, *Nightfall*, *Redemption*, *Love Child*, *Atlanta* and *Flame*, many of which have been translated into other languages and adapted for radio. She has also adapted Ingmar Bergman's *Scenes from a Marriage* for Sir Trevor Nunn. Her novels include *Truce*, *Judgement Rock* and *Sunnyside*, all published by Penguin. *Sunnyside* was also published by Viking UK. Her work has been nominated for and won many awards.

THE GIFT

JOANNA MURRAY-SMITH

CURRENCY PRESS
SYDNEY

CURRENCY PLAYS

First published in 2011
by Currency Press Pty Ltd,
PO Box 2287, Strawberry Hills, NSW, 2012, Australia
enquiries@currency.com.au
www.currency.com.au
in association with
Melbourne Theatre Company

Reprinted 2021

Copyright © Joanna Murray-Smith, 2011.

COPYING FOR EDUCATIONAL PURPOSES

The Australian *Copyright Act 1968* (Act) allows a maximum of one chapter or 10% of this book, whichever is the greater, to be copied by any educational institution for its educational purposes provided that that educational institution (or the body that administers it) has given a remuneration notice to Copyright Agency (CA) under the Act.

For details of the CA licence for educational institutions contact CA, 11/66 Goulburn Street, Sydney, NSW, 2000. Tel: 1800 066 844; email: info@copyright.com.au

COPYING FOR OTHER PURPOSES

Except as permitted under the Act, for example a fair dealing for the purposes of study, research, criticism or review, no part of this book may be reproduced, stored in a retrieval system, or transmitted in any form or by any means without prior written permission. All enquiries should be made to the publisher at the address above.

Any performance or public reading of *The Gift* is forbidden unless a licence has been received from the author or the author's agent. The purchase of this book in no way gives the purchaser the right to perform the play in public, whether by means of a staged production or a reading. All applications for public performance should be addressed to the author c/- Currency Press.

NATIONAL LIBRARY OF AUSTRALIA CIP DATA

Author:	Murray-Smith, Joanna.
Title:	The gift / Joanna Murray-Smith.
ISBN:	9780868199153 (pbk.)
Dewey Number:	A822.3

Typeset by Dean Nottle for Currency Press.
Printed by Fineline Print + Copy Services, Revesby, NSW.

Contents

To Simon Phillips

ACKNOWLEDGEMENTS

My thanks for astute criticisms and enduring faith to Raymond Gill, Simon Phillips, Aidan Fennessy and Matt Cameron.

Particular thanks to Maria Aitken, Gary Abrahams, Richard Roberts and the very talented first cast of *The Gift*, Richard Piper, Heather Bolton, Matt Dyktynski and Elizabeth Debicki for their rigorous and generous contributions in rehearsal.

Thanks to Claire Grady, Dean Nottle and all at Currency Press.

Thanks as always to Ann Tonks, Kylie McCormack and every single member of the Melbourne Theatre Company, whose professionalism and friendship makes every experience there a joy.

The Gift was first produced by Melbourne Theatre Company at The Sumner Theatre, Melbourne, on 2 June 2011 with the following cast:

ED	Richard Piper
SADIE	Heather Bolton
MARTIN	Matt Dyktynski
CHLOE	Elizabeth Debicki
WAITER	Leighton Young

Director, Maria Aitken
Set and Costume Designer, Richard Roberts
Lighting Designer, Hartley T A Kemp
Composer, Ian McDonald
Choreographer, John Bolton
Assistant Director, Gary Abrahams

CHARACTERS

ED, 50s, a self-made man
SADIE, 50s, bubbly, attractive, married to Ed
MARTIN, early-mid 30s, charismatic
CHLOE, early 30s, attractive, charismatic, married to Martin
ELEANOR, aged 4

This script went to press before the end of rehearsals and may differ from the play as performed.

ACT ONE

An expensive tropical resort. The bar. CHLOE *and* MARTIN, SADIE *and* ED. *The energy is very 'up'. They're enjoying themselves.*

CHLOE: It's true though, isn't it, you hit your thirties and you really don't need any new friends. You start out friendless and you acquire to the point of saturation and you think to yourself: *In order to be a good friend, I shouldn't take on any more. I shouldn't spread myself too thin.*

SADIE: You've made your friends.

MARTIN: Like those doctors, who close their books. Because they know that sometimes—

CHLOE: You have to be cruel to be—

ED: To be honest, we started culling friends.

MARTIN: What? You shot them?

ED: We took out a four-wheel drive with huge spotlights and we just tore around theatre foyers, school reunions, cocktail events—

SADIE: These days, that's just not funny—

ED: We got out the book and put lines through names. Red pen.

SADIE: We shouldn't be saying this—

MARTIN: Come on, we're exactly who you *should* say this stuff to—

SADIE: You know how they say: *If you haven't worn something for over a year, give it to charity, someone else could use it?*

ED: If we hadn't seen these people in over a year, we just said to ourselves:

SADIE: *They're over.*

ED: They're over.

SADIE: Sorry!

ED: There's no time. We *have* friends.

SADIE: We shouldn't be selfish—

ED: It's not nice to be selfish—

SADIE: Someone else can use them.

ED: That was the bottom line. For instance, Alison and Tony.

SADIE: Tony and Alison. There's a for instance!

ED: Someone, somewhere, needs Alison and Tony, needs to talk about the Coen brothers with them, or visit their beach house to eat Ligurian olives or give them sage advice about hydronic heating. Whatever. Someone can use more friends.

SADIE: Not us.

ED: It's selfish to keep them if there's nothing in it for us because if there's nothing in it for us, there's really nothing in it for them.

SADIE: And there *is* nothing in it for us. We shouldn't be saying this out loud.

MARTIN: What are strangers for?

CHLOE: We're no different. Only instead of being honest and putting a line through them, we just let them fall away.

MARTIN: Drop off the edge. Goodbye!

CHLOE: We don't ring.

MARTIN: Especially the ones who can't cook.

CHLOE: We leave them out of parties. We don't return their calls. And eventually, they give up. We kill off our friends by neglect.

MARTIN: If you neglect your children, you're criminal—

CHLOE: But your friends—

MARTIN: It's unpleasant, but it's not illegal.

ED: Things get to you.

MARTIN: They do, Ed. They sure do.

CHLOE: They get to us.

ED: I don't like it that Alison and Tony are such bleeding hearts.

SADIE: We're not into bleeding hearts.

ED: I don't like it that they characterise me as the right-winger because I'm not a hypocrite. I don't think that acknowledging the original landowners at public events means anything at all. It's bullshit. I don't do bullshit—

SADIE: Don't get him started—

ED: I don't like them talking about their children all the time. I like Sandra and Justin. I don't need to know the exact breakdown of their college semester, subject by subject. I don't like their car—

SADIE: We don't like status cars, even though we can personally afford an entire luxury car yard. We think it's just crass to drive a car that costs a hundred and fifty thousand dollars.

ED: It's crass.

SADIE: Crass!

ED: It's a public proclamation that one is poorly equipped.

SADIE: Edward Robert!

ED: I don't like their vague jealousy. I don't like their oriental garden.

SADIE: That's not a fault of theirs—

ED: I never said it was. It's just a fact.

SADIE: They're not Japanese.

ED: They boast about their Greenpeace donations, but they sit around on weekends torturing trees.

SADIE: It's hypocritical.

ED: I don't like the way Tony says: *Call me old-fashioned.* No-one's calling him old-fashioned.

SADIE: She overcooks beef.

ED: I don't like the way he shows off about fitness—

SADIE: She calls herself a 'perfectionist', like she's faulting herself. *I'm such a perfectionist!* Like it's dyslexia. I feel like saying: *Why don't you let me get a baseball bat and just whack it out of you?* Perfectionist!

ED: —how he runs twenty kilometres in the middle of summer. I'm fine about people being fit but talking about it bores me senseless. If you want me to admire you, make something out of nothing, make a fortune out of an idea, *show some balls*.

SADIE: I hate they way they use the word 'brunch'. I'm sorry, an 'early lunch' was good enough for our forebears—

ED: Expensive suits. Cheap shoes. That kills me.

SADIE: They still put Sade on when you come over for a drink. And it's not like they've *re*discovered her.

ED: You have to take your shoes off at their front door, because people of a higher consciousness pad around the carpet, apparently.

SADIE: Alison waits for my response and then she parrots it to everyone at book group. She has no opinions. A person needs an opinion.

ED: I don't like it that they only drink white. I mean, that's just… stupid.

SADIE: It's not superiority. It's just a slight imbalance on the friendship marketplace. Supply and demand—

ED: Demand, supply. We are slightly more in demand than Tony and Alison. That's not their fault.

SADIE: But it's not our fault either.

ED: It's not about superiority—

SADIE: Well, a bit—

ED: It's a little bit about feeling superior—

CHLOE: If it's not real, if it's not *authentic*, then cut the friendship loose.

SADIE: Tough but true.

ED: You're our first real friends for a decade.

MARTIN: We feel the same way.

SADIE: Will you have us?

CHLOE: Will you have us?

Beat. Lights. Time jump.

To the audience:

SADIE: We'd been having a few problems, nothing major, and I wasn't stupid, I knew a holiday wouldn't make them disappear, but I didn't think it would hurt. I'm fully aware that it's just about impossible to ever, ever get back to who we were when Ed started the first store and we fell in love. Boring, boring story. The same the world over. Middle-aged couples who started out poor and in absolute lust with each other, make some dough and end up *in like* with each other. It felt—it felt—as if something was missing. All that money, money we never dreamt we'd have and all we really wanted was to recapture something of the mystery and the electricity and the danger. I booked it for our twenty-fifth wedding anniversary. I figured if it's good enough for the Sarkozys, it's good enough for us. Someone said The Sea Temple had good bed linen and personal butlers. I'd read about it in *Gourmet Traveller.*

To each other:

ED: I like my butlers impersonal.

SADIE: It's a thousand a night. You get a butler. You want to sack the butler?

ED: I don't want to sack the butler. I don't know the butler.

SADIE: I'll have them sack the butler if you wish.

ED: Don't sack the butler.

SADIE: Your call, Mr Egalitarian. [*To the audience*] It was nice.

ED: [*to the audience*] It was hot. It was nice. A half bottle of Bubbles de France in the minibar fridge cost ninety-five dollars. The Pringles were nine bucks.

SADIE: I want a chip!

ED: [*to* SADIE] I don't like being taken for a ride.

SADIE: Sell a horse. [*To the audience*] We ate every night at the in-house restaurant, overlooking the beach. Candlelight. Sea breeze. A sulky young pianist with large breasts covering 'classics' that were written sometime in the last eighteen months.

ED: Very, very nice breasts. Very nice. And quite a nice voice.

SADIE: [*to the audience*] We noticed this other couple that had arrived the day after us. You know how you notice other couples, because well, basically, you're captive. You've eaten the fusion prawn dish four nights in a row, you've had the massage, you've had the free beach crafts tuition, you've been for a kayak and a romantic picnic on a deserted beach on an outlying island and now the only thing left is to watch other human beings, like you're at the zoo. At the zoo for rich people just like you. People who can afford to go tracking ancient civilisations in the Amazon, but would rather sleep in a Heavenly bed and order gin-slings from a personal butler.

ED: It's not PC but it's what we like.

SADIE: It's very uncool. And no doubt full of carbon emissions. I'm sure we have a footprint the size of a yeti. But we like it. [*To* ED] I'll have the warm salad of limpet and yak's cheese.

ED: Let's see… I think I'll have the fusion prawns.

SADIE: [*to the audience*] It was the actual night of our anniversary. Twenty-five years.

ED: I could have the duck with quail egg tortellini or the wild asparagus with shredded otter and coriander… Have you ever had otter?

SADIE: I think I had it once at that place with the Antons. It was like chewy chicken.

ED: Why bother if it's like chicken?

SADIE: The chicken's a reference point.

ED: No, I'll have the prawns.

SADIE: Again?

ED: Prawns with lima bean fudge, marsala, dukkah and crushed pomegranates. Who knew?

SADIE: I never crushed a pomegranate, ever. What about the steak with chocolate and tagine of squid ink?

ED: I think I'll stick with the prawns.

To the audience:

SADIE: We noticed the other couple were having the seafood platter to share.

Lights up on CHLOE *and* MARTIN *at another table.*

CHLOE *laughs.*

She was laughing. I remember she was laughing because I wondered how does she keep her laughter fresh? Is he a comedian? Have I seen him on a talk show?

ED: I just noticed her legs.

SADIE: She did have good legs.

ED: I'm usually a breast man but I take pleasure where I can get it.

SADIE: [*to* ED] Between the breasts of the pianist and the legs of the guest, you had quite a buffet of body parts.

ED: Funny.

To the audience:

SADIE: There was something attractive about them and something very… I don't know… bonded. They were pleased to be in each other's company and their happiness somehow… well, it might have been irritating, but it wasn't. I thought if she can laugh like that, well, [*to* ED] *you* can be funny—

ED: I am funny.

To the audience:

SADIE: Ed's quite funny.

ED: I'm 'the funny one'.

SADIE: He's quite amusing.

ED: Amongst our friends.

SADIE: I could probably laugh like that if he and I—if we—

ED: I love her. I'm crazy about her, but—

SADIE: I adore him. I do. But sometimes it's as if—

ED: As if we're just waiting for something to happen.

SADIE: Then the waiter brought them a cake with a big plaque on it saying 'Congratulations on Eight Years'.

ED: It had sparklers.

SADIE: We didn't have a cake. Ed never mentioned it to the waiter when he made the reservation.

ED: Sadie never mentioned it when she booked the villa.

SADIE: After the sparklers stopped fizzing, she took them out of the cake and they kissed and everyone in the restaurant clapped. Us too.

ED: A slightly awkward moment.

SADIE: Because, you know, after a while, in a marriage—

ED: You eschew romance. Romance is for kiddies. Little notes on pillows? Rose petals scattered on the bed? Give me a fucking break. It's phony. I don't do phony.

SADIE: But even so—

ED: Sometimes, perhaps, it's not a bad idea to fake it.

SADIE: Sometimes a phony gesture is better than no gesture at all.

ED *stands.*

[*To* ED] Sit down!

ED *clears his throat.*

ED: [*to the restaurant*] Excuse me!

SADIE: Sit the fuck down, Ed!

ED: [*to the restaurant*] It's been twenty-five years of marital bliss for us. Twenty-five years since this little lady agreed to have me for better or worse but not for lunch.

SADIE: Please, earth, swallow me up. Pull me down, down, into the Caribbean mudflats, down beneath the basalt whatever, past the coral and the pretty fish, down into the dark, dark depths where the amoebas swim on the ocean floor.

Addressing the audience:

ED: The crowd cheered.

SADIE: There was a polite smattering of applause.

ED: I'm not bad at public speaking, if I say so myself. And I do.

SADIE: Then the other couple looked over at us, raising their glasses.

CHLOE *and* MARTIN *do so.*

ED: They looked so tanned and attractive.

SADIE: They gave tanning a good name. Again.

ED: Nice-looking people. She with the very shapely legs.

SADIE: We raised our glasses.

SADIE *and* ED *do so.*

ED: They yelled:

MARTIN/CHLOE: Mind if we join you?

SADIE: I didn't want them to join us but it was either that or sit in silence with Ed. Not that I mind sitting in silence. It's very nice. It's 'companionable'. And it's quiet. But you're a long time dead, as the saying goes. [*To* CHLOE *and* MARTIN] Please do!

MARTIN *and* CHLOE *approach.* ED *and* SADIE *stand.*

SADIE/ED/MARTIN/CHLOE: [*to each other*] Congratulations!

They all laugh.

ED: [*introducing*] Ed, Sadie.

CHLOE: [*and back*] Chloe, Martin.

ED: Pull up a pew.

They all sit.

SADIE: How long have you—?

CHLOE: Four days—

ED: We got here Monday—

MARTIN: Okay, we got in Tuesday—

SADIE: Home next Tuesday—

CHLOE: Us too!

SADIE: Lovely, isn't it—?

MARTIN: Oh, it's lovely—

CHLOE: It's a lovely place—

ED: The prawns are delicious—

MARTIN: Minibar's a bit steep—

ED: Charge like wounded bulls, Martin!

MARTIN: Captive market, isn't it, Ed?

ED: Nine-dollar Pringles. It's a travesty.

MARTIN: Over the top.

ED: Completely over the top but you have let it go.

MARTIN: So true.

ED: What's the point of looking at that view, sitting in your private outdoor plunge pool festooned in frangipani at sunset and feeling enraged about the Pringles?

MARTIN: No point. Let it go. Let the thought sail into that sunset.

CHLOE: Are you from—?

SADIE: Can't you tell? All style no substance.

They all laugh.

MARTIN: We're from—

ED: We knew when we saw you.

They all laugh.

ED/SADIE/MARTIN/CHLOE: Lovely night! [*Laughing*] Oh!

SADIE: How was the seafood platter?

CHLOE: Very fresh.

SADIE: The seafood is so fresh here.

MARTIN: Incredibly fresh.

ED: I don't think I've ever had such fresh seafood.

SADIE: Right out of the ocean.

ED: That's generally where seafood comes from, pet.

MARTIN: So what line are you in, Ed?

ED: Snaposquinters.

MARTIN: Wow.

CHLOE: Excuse my ignorance—

ED: No, listen—

SADIE: No-one knows. *I* didn't know.

ED: Been in Snaposquinters for a long time now. I was at the forefront, actually.

SADIE: He was at the forefront of Snaposquinters when other people were backpedalling, on the back foot, behind the eight ball.

MARTIN: Snapo—?

SADIE: You know when you secure your seatbelt and something clicks, locks it into place, that clicking thing.

CHLOE: My God, that's—

MARTIN: That's a Snaposquinter?

Beat.

ED: We're kidding.

Beat as CHLOE *and* MARTIN *catch up.*

SADIE: It's a little routine that we do!

CHLOE: Oh!

ED: I make something up and—

SADIE: I run with it. It's juvenile.

CHLOE: You had us going there!

SADIE: Woodworking machinery.

MARTIN: Woodworking machinery?

ED: That's right. 'Back From the Edgebander'.

MARTIN: What?

SADIE: 'Back From the Edgebander'.

CHLOE: Oh, that late night ad! The shirtless guys in the overalls, singing that song.

MARTIN: That's a franchise, isn't it?

ED: Seventy stores throughout the Pacific, including Samoa. Thirty-three in the US and growing.

MARTIN: Including Samoa!

SADIE: He's proud of Samoa.

CHLOE: And why not?!

ED: Never thought it would become what it has, but there it is.

CHLOE: I thought you might be an optometrist.

ED: Really?

CHLOE: Thought you could fix my Snaposquint.

They all laugh.

ED: [*to* MARTIN] She's good!

CHLOE: Oh!

ED: Funny!

MARTIN: And what about you, Sadie?

SADIE: Oh, I facilitate his greatness.

They all laugh.

No, I actually do.

ED: She's funny, too. It's great when women are funny. There are so many women comedians now, have you noticed, Martin? Once upon a time, there was Lucille Ball. Now there's one on every corner.

SADIE: A long time ago, I did secretarial work, but I gave it up.

ED: Some men don't think women are funny, but they have a natural gift. In my observation.

CHLOE: Do you miss working, Sadie?

SADIE: Oh, I've found that I'm much better at spending money than making it. I think it's important to go where your talents lie.

ED: She's gifted.

CHLOE: Kids?

SADIE: No. No children. I really should go back to work but—

ED: It's a full-time job being my other half!

SADIE: Sometimes I think I'm his other three quarters!

They all laugh.

ED: See what I mean?

SADIE: What about you two?

CHLOE: We're both from the city. Born and raised.

SADIE. How did you two—?

ED: Here we go, the inquisition!

CHLOE: Our parents knew each other—

ED: Sweethearts!

CHLOE: He never looked at me—

ED: Hard to get.

CHLOE: He was too handsome.

MARTIN: Not so!

CHLOE: And vain. And unreachable. I knew at sixteen that I had to give him ten years to realise. Then we didn't see each other for nearly that long.

MARTIN: I'm a slow learner.

CHLOE: I'm a journalist.

SADIE: I knew you were brainy! I said to Ed: *She looks brainy*, didn't I, Ed? It's a sixth sense.

CHLOE: Oh, I don't know—

SADIE: I'm very intuitive, aren't I, Ed?

ED: Definitely, doll.

MARTIN: She was the youngest contributor to *Artforum* in its history. Her PhD was excerpted in the *Herald Tribune*. She thinks like an intellectual and writes like a poet.

CHLOE: Oh, babe!

SADIE: Oh, that's what Ed says about me, don't you, honey?

ED: Daily.

SADIE: Gosh. Clever girl!

ED: You went for the job interview and he was your editor?

MARTIN: I'm an artist.

ED: An artist.

MARTIN: That's right.

ED: That's your actual job?

MARTIN: U-huh.

ED: An artist?

MARTIN: Ah… yes.

Beat.

SADIE: Wow.

Beat.

MARTIN: She came to interview me.

ED: Interview in quotation marks.

CHLOE: I really did interview him. For *Artforum*. I said: *If you feel me up, I'll call you the hot new thing!*

They all laugh.

SADIE: Oh, you arty types!

ED: You stand around all day making… art?

MARTIN: That's right.

ED: That's how you make a living?

MARTIN: For better or worse. Usually, worse!

ED: You make art?

MARTIN: U-huh.

ED: Gee.

MARTIN: We-ll—

ED: An artist.

MARTIN: Yep.

SADIE: Sometimes I think there's just this invisible line drawn right through the population. The ones that seize life in, in—

CHLOE: All its infinite strangeness—

SADIE: Bingo! The ones who embrace it in all its infinite strangeness—and the ones who read about it.

MARTIN: Oh, Sadie. You look as if you've been around the block a couple of times!

SADIE: Oh, I've been around the block, Martin.

MARTIN: Not *our* block, though.

SADIE: No, Martin, you're right. The block I've been around is full of boring fancy houses full of boring fancy people who pay other people to mow their lawns and cook their meals and raise their kids. That's my block. Where the adults are out buying Porsche Cayennes and the kids are out there getting their nipples pierced. Honestly, if I'd gone out at sixteen and pierced my nipple, there'd have been hell to pay.

ED: There was very little talk of nipples in those days. Let alone accessorising them.

SADIE: It's no way to raise a child.

ED: Suddenly, she's a revolutionary!

Laughter.

SADIE: He's funny.

ED: Excuse me, Che, could you pass the vino?

More laughter. SADIE *passes the wine.*

So you just pop on your beret of a morning, Marty, and whip out the old easel?

CHLOE: Martin's not a painter—

SADIE: You're not a painter, Martin?

MARTIN: Can't paint to save my life!

CHLOE: Martin's a conceptual artist.

SADIE: Well, *excuse me*! A *conceptual* artist, if you don't mind!

ED: What *is* a conceptual artist?

CHLOE: An artist who puts the idea of the work at a higher level than how it looks or what it's composed from. Le Witt said: *The idea becomes a machine that makes the art.*

ED: Le Witt wasn't very witty, was he?

MARTIN: [s*lightly irritated*] This is rivetting. Chloe—

CHLOE: That said, Martin's work is very beautiful.

ED *moves to pour* MARTIN *another drink..*

MARTIN: No more for me, Ed. I think I'll hit the sack, actually.

SADIE: Oh Martin, really?

CHLOE: Oh Martin, come on—

ED: We're just getting cosy—

CHLOE: [*bothered*] Don't be boring, honey—

MARTIN: I'm sure Sadie and Ed don't want to hear about Martin-The-Potential-Genius, Chlo—

SADIE: But we *do*, Martin!

CHLOE: They do, Martin!

ED: Of course we do. We want to know everything.

Beat.

CHLOE: [*plaintive, slightly flirtatious*] Babe?

Beat.

MARTIN: One more then.

SADIE: [*clapping*] Oh, yippee!

ED fills his glass.

ED: My old dad used to say, concentrate on what people can't do without. Because that's your bottom line. Some things you can do without, but you can't do without woodworking machinery.

MARTIN: Smart man, your dad.

ED: People can do without art though, can't they? I mean, you can just have a wall. The wall you can't do without. What's *on* the wall is an optional extra.

MARTIN: Some people can't live without art. Mad but true.

CHLOE: Thank God!

ED: This might seem a silly question but how do you know what art to make? How do you build a market, Martin?

MARTIN: It's not a business that serves the market. Well, of course it does. Of course there is a market: a vast, hungry market. But the art itself has to stay… innocent.

ED: Innocent?

MARTIN: If I chase the market, I'll lose whatever it likes about me. What makes an artist popular is sometimes their disdain for popularity.

A beat while they ponder this.

SADIE: Of course you probably don't *choose* art, do you, Martin? Like marine biology or, or cheese-making.

ED: Cheese-making?

SADIE: Some people choose to make cheese, Ed. That's a fact.

MARTIN: You're right, Sadie. *It* chooses *you.*

ED: Like the priesthood.

CHLOE: Exactly. And artists pray a lot, too. For divine inspiration.

MARTIN: Alcohol helps.

ED: Alcohol helps!

SADIE: Alcohol helps! But seriously—

MARTIN: This can't be interesting!

CHLOE: Martin, come on. Ed and Sadie are asking you to explain—

MARTIN: I can't explain. [*Not rude*] Actually, I don't *want* to explain.

ED: I'm interested, Martin. No bullshit.

MARTIN: Another day. Ed—

ED: Come on, Martin.

SADIE: It's fascinating, Martin—

ED: No bullshit, buddy. This is all news to me.

Beat as MARTIN *thinks, then resolves to give them what they want.*

MARTIN: Alright, then. Okay. It's just about finding the world inside your head a little more compelling. It's hard to leave it. You become wedded to hypotheses. You don't look at the world and say: *This is how it is.* You say: *How might it be? And how do I share a... well, a wondrous thought?*

CHLOE: A wondrous thought.

MARTIN: You have a shimmering thought that won't let you go and you think: How do I share that?

SADIE: My thoughts never shimmer. Mine just… sit there.

MARTIN: I don't think it is a choice, Ed. I question whether I'm a good artist or a bad artist every day, but I *am* an artist. It's not a choice, no. It's blind faith.

ED: I hear you.

MARTIN: Do you, Ed?

ED: Loud and clear. I wake up in the morning and take the world in. In my own way. And it never occurs to me: *How might it be?*

SADIE: I envy you because you two live in the world of big ideas.

CHLOE: Oh, come on, Sadie—

SADIE: No. You do. And I've never had a big idea in my life. It feels good finally confessing it.

ED: She's not a big ideas person. She's right on the money there.

SADIE: Oh, I'd like to be.

ED: We'd all like to be. That's not the issue.

SADIE: The arts!

ED: We like the arts. To a point.

MARTIN: Us too.

SADIE: You are funny!

ED: We're not complete philistines. I love the Impressionists.

SADIE: We both love the Impressionists.

ED: The one in Paris with the Impressionists, we make a bee-line for. And there's a little joint across the road with seriously good chocolate éclairs. You can't have too many Impressionists.

SADIE: There are quite a lot.

ED: There certainly are.

SADIE: Amazing what they did with a dot.

ED: Not *too* many though, never too many.

CHLOE: Very true.

SADIE: It's hard to remember which one did the water lilies, isn't it? Confess! So I do a little trick. I think Manet has an 'a' which is in the word 'water lilies'. But Monet doesn't have an 'a'. So think of the artist that has the 'a' like water lilies has an 'a', and then it's the *other* one.

Beat.

ED: Sadie goes to the ballet. And we go to the theatre every so often.

SADIE: Once in a while. We saw—

ED: We saw a show not that long ago—

SADIE: *Wicked*. Not Shakespeare, but it's great fun.

ED: It's a hoot.

SADIE: Oh, you youngies—you probably think that's awfully 'mainstream'!

CHLOE: Not at all—

SADIE: I'm sure there are lots of interesting things happening in… in Europe… that Ed and I know nothing about. There are probably theatre companies of… of dwarves…

CHLOE: Yes, there are, Sadie.

ED: Of dwarves?

MARTIN: We saw a show last year. It was really very good. *A Doll's House*.

ED: You have to be kidding?

CHLOE: No, actually. No, we're not.

ED: What? Lots of little… people, little people in costumes, tiny little people in a doll's house?

MARTIN: Exactly.

They laugh. Beat. SADIE *addresses the audience.*

SADIE: Frankly, they had come along at just the right time. Two people in a long marriage can find they say just what the other person *expects* them to say. Like you're two people doing a thirty-year routine: same observations, same jokes, just samey-samey. Suddenly we had these two handsome young people in our midst who had this *energy*. I think just being there with them was giving Ed and me a sense of… escape.

SADIE *turns back to the others.*

MARTIN: It's actually very relaxing not being— Well. This isn't our usual—

ED: Not resorty types?

CHLOE: Oh, we'd like to be but—

SADIE: You google and there are hundreds, aren't there? Even when you tick your must-haves, there are still hundreds. I suppose one goes on a personal recommendation or a sense that a particular resort has the x factor. I'm a great believer in the x factor.

ED: You know what you're getting. Hyatts, Hiltons, whatnot, you're buying peace of mind, aren't you? It might not be astonishing, but maybe 'astonishing' is not as good as 'reliable' and 'consistent'. Consistency is very underrated.

SADIE: [*directed to* MARTIN] Although the x factor has some influence, I find.

ED: We came here to relax—

SADIE: Relax. Yes. But also—

ED: Unwind.

SADIE: But to be honest, we also hope—

ED: Sometimes we feel as if something's—

SADIE: That was part of what we wanted—wasn't it?

ED: Hoping it might spice things up a bit.

SADIE: He's saying I—

ED: Not you. Not you—

SADIE: I'm predictable.

ED: Did I say that?

CHLOE: He didn't say that.

ED: Did I say it?

MARTIN: No, Ed, you didn't say that.

SADIE: I'm predictable.

ED: I didn't—

CHLOE: He didn't—

SADIE: [*no offence taken*] I'm predictable. I'm a predictable person. You know what you've got with me.

MARTIN: He never—

CHLOE: Really, he—

SADIE: I'm exactly what you expect.

ED: You're predictable.

SADIE: Exactly.

ED: You said it, baby.

SADIE: I'm thoroughly predictable, apparently. I'm a safe bet. I'm a sure thing. Not astonishing but reliable. Like a Hyatt.

ED: There are worse things.

SADIE: I'm not a Holiday Inn.

ED: Exactly.

SADIE: I'm not a Travelodge.

ED: I think we have that now.

SADIE: I hope I'm not speaking out of turn. But Ed and I have spent more of our life together than alone. Something—something changes when you—when that happens.

ED: [*embarrassed*] Too much info, doll!

CHLOE: Go on, Sadie.

SADIE: Maybe it would have been different if we'd— Well, children change everything, don't they? I think… the joy of that… Well, come what may, you share that child. That child is both of you and something absolutely itself. I think that if you woke up every morning looking at this human you made, you'd—well, the miracle of that would somehow overcome the—the boredom.

ED: Alright, Sadie—

SADIE: At a certain point in a marriage, there's this tiny voice inside you that pipes up: *Who was I?*

CHLOE: Who was I?

SADIE: Who was I? [*Beat.*] We're here to get something back.

ED: Our space.

SADIE: Look at each other and say: *Hello You!*

ED: Not just: *Oh, it's you.*

Beat.

MARTIN: We won it.

ED/SADIE: What?

MARTIN: This trip. A raffle.

CHLOE: Little girl next door selling tickets for cerebral palsy.

SADIE: Oh, I'm a great believer in karma. Aren't I, Ed?

MARTIN: At first we felt a little embarrassed—

CHLOE: Our friends, you see, they're—

MARTIN: Artists struggle. We struggle.

SADIE: Do you struggle?

MARTIN: I'm afraid we do, Sadie.

SADIE: Oh, but when you're an artist, it's important to struggle. I mean, if you didn't struggle, the work wouldn't be any good.

MARTIN: I'd rather not struggle, actually.

CHLOE: Things are looking hopeful—

MARTIN: That's true—

CHLOE: His pieces are very big. You don't buy them on impulse.

MARTIN: Very big. Installations.

ED: Pricey, Marty?

MARTIN: Pretty pricey, Ed.

CHLOE: And rather edgy. Not impulse buys.

ED: There are more things in life than money. I'm no more interesting than I used to be when I had none. Money hasn't made me more interesting, has it, Sadie?

SADIE: Definitely not.

ED: It can't buy you height.

SADIE: No. That's out.

ED: It doesn't buy you personality.

CHLOE: No, but it buys you a dishwasher.

ED: Do you want a dishwasher, Chloe?

CHLOE: Yes, I do.

ED: I'll buy you one!

CHLOE: Don't be ridiculous!

ED: Let me! Let me buy you a dishwasher!

CHLOE: I can't let a strange man buy me a dishwasher!

SADIE: A strange man!

MARTIN: Oh, twenty paces at dawn, Ed!

ED: Twenty paces at dawn!

CHLOE: You might want me to bend over and stack it!

SADIE: Bend over and stack it!

Beat. Laughter. All enjoying the fun.

ED: I'm relaxed.

SADIE: I'm relaxed.

ED: It suddenly all seems very relaxing. All's we need is some good jazz—

CHLOE: Oh, Martin's a jazz nut—

MARTIN: [*to* ED] You like jazz?

ED: No, I'm insane about jazz.

MARTIN: Who do you listen to?

ED: A lot of old stuff, mostly. Miles. Ornette.

MARTIN: You'd be interested in something I picked up last year. An original 1959 pressing of *The Shape of Jazz to Come.*

ED: You. Are. Kidding. Me.

MARTIN: Nope.

ED: I have that!

MARTIN: You have it?

ED: I've never met anyone with that!

MARTIN: I've also got *The Black Saint and the Sinner Lady*—

ED: Mingus. Jesus. 1963.

SADIE: Here we go!

ED: I'm ordering another bottle. Something special. Something that costs the GDP of the entire country.

CHLOE: Oh, well—

ED: This is what I love to do—

SADIE: He loves to do this— He's a wine bore—

ED: I'm a bit of a wine bore—

MARTIN: I aspire—

ED: I wanted to go into— We nearly—

SADIE: Oh, Lord—a hobby farm—but—

ED: Horses or grapes—

SADIE: There really isn't room for both. Even with a full-time domestic slave—

ED: Slave to spending!

SADIE: I like clothes.

CHLOE: I love clothes.

ED: Grapes or horses, horses or grapes. But not both.

SADIE: We have a stud.

ED: Eighty-five minutes door to door.

SADIE: The farm started out little and it's got big.

ED: I've got good people.

SADIE: Good people! Excuse me, King of Samoa.

ED: Princess Gaia.

MARTIN: She's your filly?

ED: We're doing alright. Life is good. Isn't it?

MARTIN: We think so.

CHLOE: Life is good!

SADIE: Every so often you think it, but you don't dare to say it in case we're struck down—

CHLOE: Sometimes you need to give thanks.

ED: We grumble about all the bad things, all the irritants, all the catastrophes looming, the global warming, the disease and misfortune, the earthquakes, the bouts of irrational sadness, the rednecks, the neo Nazis, the suicide bombers, the polluters, the corrupt leaders, the starving people, the rioters, the fallen rain forests, malaria, war orphans, the disappearing Amazonian twinkle fish. But sometimes, please can we—do we have to care all the time, do we have to tap into the full horror 24/7? Can we not, sometimes, just *repress*—?

Beat.

MARTIN: To friendship.

They raise their glasses.

Light change.

To the audience:

SADIE: The more they talked, the more attractive they were. They were both lovely-looking, not just handsome but… lit up. And there was this optimism about them that was… enchanting. They weren't… disappointed. I don't even know how to— It was refreshing to meet people poorer than us. I looked at Martin and I saw a glimmer of Edward Robert Dunbar as a young man. Alive to his own potential.

Light change. As they were.

To each other:

MARTIN: Very hands-on still, are you, Ed?

ED: I'm a bit of a control freak, Martin.

SADIE: Just a bit!

ED: I try to delegate now, but just when you decide to leave it up to someone else, they disappoint you.

SADIE: He can't let go.

ED: I can let go.

SADIE: You can't let go.

ED: I don't want to let go.

SADIE: You can't let go because it's your life. It's his life.

ED: I've got young people working for me with MBAs. Years they've spent in universities 'learning' about business. Let me tell you, they don't know a thing about people and if you don't know a thing about people, you don't know a thing about business.

CHLOE: I bet that's true.

ED: We need to be getting these kids out of the cloistered classrooms and into the real world.

MARTIN: I have to confess, I saw you by the pool yesterday—

SADIE: Oh, we saw you, too! Funny.

MARTIN: You were reading the Bill Gates biography.

ED: I don't see the point of fiction.

SADIE: Oh, sayonara *War and Peace*!

MARTIN: [*surprised*] I love biographies, too.

CHLOE: We play this game where we guess what strangers do, who they are, where they live, star signs, all kinds of naughty things—favourite positions—

SADIE: Oh, my Lord!

CHLOE: And Martin said: *Business*.

SADIE: No!

ED: Is it that obvious?

SADIE: You had us pegged! Did you guess: *Swinging from the chandeliers*?

CHLOE: Favourite position! Exactly!

ED: After twenty-five years, it's more like *cleaning* the chandeliers.

They all laugh.

So how did you pick me, Martin, if you don't mind me asking?

Beat.

MARTIN: They're all a little drunk. You're at peace with your place in the universe. You've put your stamp on it. That's the mark of a man who has made his own way and can measure his success plainly, in dollar terms, if you like. Every day you face the peculiar, belligerent force of the marketplace. Economies rise and fall. They're like tides. And you have to roll with the tides of chance. You survive or you go under. It takes courage and, usually, brains.

CHLOE: Woodworking machinery. There's actually something rather poetic about that. It's real stuff, isn't it? It's the stuff of life. Wood. Jesus was a carpenter, after all.

ED: All true.

MARTIN: The rest of us like to believe we control circumstances while you—well, you live quite happily knowing that circumstances befall us and we must manage them as best we can. So many come undone when they are forced to acknowledge that life happens *to* them. But you take it in your stride: the catastrophic implications of being alive.

SADIE: Hallelujah!

ED: I never realised why I was so cheerful!

MARTIN: Glad to be of service!

SADIE: I just love the way you speak, Martin! It's so Black. So Martin Luther King! 'To Dream the Impossible Dream' and all that.

ED: That was Andy Williams, Sadie. Martin Luther King was 'I *have* a dream'.

SADIE: Well, you know.

ED: Not often confused, those two.

SADIE: Well, I'm not sure it's Ed who's alive to the catastrophic implications! I mean, it's people like Martin who make the universe shake for mere mortals like us. I can tell you're going to be a star, Martin.

MARTIN: Thanks for the vote of confidence, Sadie.

SADIE: You've got that glow! Hasn't he, Ed? He's just got a glow! An aura!

MARTIN: I've always wanted an aura—

CHLOE: Some of the major private collections are sniffing around. Martin plays tennis with a friend of the guy at the Tate Modern.

SADIE: Oh, we went to London a couple of years ago. Conference. We did go to the Tate Modern—it had an ear in the foyer—

ED: It was a trumpet. A giant trumpet.

SADIE: It looked like a trumpet or an ear, but I think it was a vagina.

ED: It was a trumpet. I'd know a vagina.

SADIE: 'I'd know a vagina'! It wasn't *my* vagina. As far as I know!

They all laugh.

[*To the audience*] We went to the bar and drank mojitos until late. Over those limy, minty, zingy cocktails, something clicked. I thought we could learn something from these people. They were switched on to life in some very attractive way. I always like it when couples show admiration for one another. Admiration is something that seems to have been hijacked as if it has to be reserved for people we don't know very well. When you see it between lovers, it's very touching.

To each other:

ED: Well, Confession Time. I have a real problem with that stuff, Marty. The kind of art that tells you it's cleverer than you are. To me, that's just grandstanding. I don't think it's art.

SADIE: Do we care, Ed?

CHLOE: Plenty would agree with you, Ed.

ED: I look at some of this modern stuff and I'm thinking, this is just about the Big Sell.

SADIE: Don't be embarrassing.

CHLOE: Often it is.

ED: It's just an edgebander with a bit of froth and bubble.

SADIE: Why don't you pipe down, Mr Art Expert?

MARTIN: Oh, there are artists like that, Ed. You're bang on the money.

SADIE: But you're not, Martin.

CHLOE: He's not.

SADIE: Of course he isn't.

MARTIN: I hope I'm not.

ED: I'm sure you'll persuade me.

CHLOE: Oh, he will, Ed. He'll blow your mind.

SADIE: Ed is just frightened of things he doesn't understand. You're just not on that wavelength—

ED: On which wavelength?

SADIE: On the art wavelength. It's not your wavelength.

ED: What is my wavelength?

SADIE: The golf wavelength.

CHLOE: Anyway, the Tate Modern guy—

MARTIN: Todd Bunbridge-Hoffman—

CHLOE: He's coming to see the next installation—

MARTIN: Couple of weeks—

CHLOE: Martin's opening—

MARTIN: Bunbridge-Hoffman is curating—

CHLOE: 'I've got the power to make or break'—

MARTIN: Not a huge sense of humour, apparently, which is a worry—

CHLOE: They're doing a show called 'Overtaking Jesus'. Interesting contemporary artists over the age of thirty-three. They're looking for a couple of late additions.

MARTIN: I'm a candidate, but who knows?

CHLOE: Martin is just peeking over the fence into the big time.

MARTIN: Oh, Chloe is talking me up.

CHLOE: Not at all. He's brilliant.

ED: 'Overtaking Jesus'. So much for modesty—

CHLOE: It's a real shot at the big time. He is absolutely brilliant. He has a mind like—the way he reinterprets— Martin's the most interesting person I know.

SADIE: Oh. That is just lovely.

MARTIN: Ultimately, we're at the mercy of someone else's taste. It's an exhausting place to be but that's how it is if you create.

SADIE: What is the Big Time, Chloe?

CHLOE: The big time is this wide green lawn. Sparkling green underneath a bright blue sky, a huge green lawn tended to by Todd Bunbridge-Hoffman. Todd Bunbridge-Hoffman is standing there in the middle of this wide green lawn. It's beautiful there. There are lovely, well-dressed people standing on it. It's paradise.

ED: You never call me 'brilliant', Sadie.

SADIE: [*a tiny beat*] No.

CHLOE: For Martin, art is something personal… it's a personal inquiry, something… fearless and forensic. It's not just an act of provocation. It's very—human.

Beat as they take this in. MARTIN *tenderly touches her hand.*

Martin's installation already has quite a buzz around it.

MARTIN: There's a bit of a buzz.

ED: What does it look like?

CHLOE: Oh!

SADIE: 'What does it look like?'!

ED: What do you see?

SADIE: 'What do you see?'!

CHLOE: No, Sadie, it's a perfectly reasonable question.

MARTIN: It's a glass box.

ED: A glass box?

MARTIN: Yes.

ED: A small glass box?

MARTIN: A big glass box.

ED: A big glass box?

MARTIN: Yes.

ED: Do you make the box?

MARTIN: I have the box made.

ED: Someone else makes the box?

MARTIN: I have excellent people who make the box.

ED: So if *they* make the box—

MARTIN: Yes.

ED: What do *you* do?

MARTIN: Well I… I *think* of the box.

ED: Right.

SADIE: Anyone can make a box. Thinking of a box is the hard part.

ED: Is there anything in the box?

SADIE: You don't have to have something in a box to 'validate' the box, Ed! Good Lord!

MARTIN: Actually there is, Sadie. There *is* something in the box. A child.

ED: There's a child in the box?

MARTIN: That's right.

ED: Is it a real child?

MARTIN: It's a child made from light. She looks as if she's made from vapour, but it's actually light.

SADIE: Wow.

ED: What does it mean, Martin?

SADIE: 'What does it mean?' Honestly. It's not a cordless drill.

ED: I'd like Martin to tell me what it means.

MARTIN: Well, I could tell you, Ed, but then I'd have to kill you.

SADIE: 'Have to kill you'! Hilarious.

MARTIN: It means what you give it to mean, Ed. Like most art.

CHLOE: In receiving it, you complete it. *You* give it its meaning. When you think about it, Ed, each of us bestows a kind of narrative on the world around us. Our presence alters it. It's not the same before us as it is when we pass through.

MARTIN: We shake up the air. Art works in the same way. 'Meaning'? It's an improvisation.

ED: Like jazz, isn't it?

MARTIN: Exactly, Ed.

ED: That glass box is your version of Ornette Coleman's *The Shape of Jazz To Come*.

MARTIN: Appreciating art is really just... about temporarily suspending doubt.

ED: Doubt?

MARTIN: Yes.

ED: Suspending doubt?

MARTIN: Things happen when we suspend doubt.

CHLOE: We unpeel the layers of preconceptions and inheritance and prejudice. We acknowledge our own limitations and long to be surprised.

MARTIN: Surprise. It's everything.

CHLOE: It gives us... grandeur. When doubt goes, life... expands. Things come our way. Instead of closing our eyes. We say: *Take me.*

MARTIN: These moments are our choreographers.

SADIE: Gosh.

ED: I guess that's— Remember, Sadie—

SADIE: I know what you're going—

ED: But it's an example—

SADIE: He changed trains at the last minute. At the last minute he took the twelve-fifteen instead of the nine-fifteen.

ED: Food poisoning. Tuna roll. I missed the nine-fifteen so I took the twelve-fifteen.

SADIE: We sat next to each other and the rest is history.

ED: Who would I have married if I ate the hot dog?

SADIE: George Clooney might have taken your seat if you'd stayed on the nine-fifteen!

ED: He's gay.

SADIE: He's not gay.

ED: He's gay.

SADIE: George is not gay

ED: He has a villa at Lake Como with gold cupids on the ceiling.

Beat.

SADIE: Jude Law might have taken your seat. That could have been *my* moment that changed everything.

CHLOE: We have the public reminders. The parents who left their little girl in the hotel room while they had dinner only two hundred yards away with friends. The janitor who changed his roster to be in the World Trade Centre on 9/11.

MARTIN: But all of us are living a narrative in which a chance encounter or moment becomes the author of our future.

SADIE: Gosh.

ED: And what was yours, Martin?

MARTIN: Well. [*Beat.*] Actually, it was having my way with Chloe one night on the kitchen table after a tequila party and that particular, ironman, obstinate sperm went sailing headlong towards that very accommodating egg.

SADIE: You have kids! My God!

CHLOE: Just one.

MARTIN: Eleanor. She's four.

SADIE: Eleanor! How lovely.

ED: Is she here?

MARTIN: She's at home. With friends.

SADIE: You have to make time, don't you—?

CHLOE: You have to—

SADIE: For just you.

ED: Bet she's a looker.

MARTIN: Big green eyes and a certain twinkle.

CHLOE: Definitely a twinkle.

SADIE: Oh, a twinkle!

CHLOE: She is lovely. But little girls! It's genetically programmed—

SADIE: Clothes?

CHLOE: Insists on dressing herself and the hair has to be 'just so'.

MARTIN: Every morning there's a hair issue. Has to be plaits. Has to be pigtails. Has to have ribbons.

ED: Just like Sadie!

SADIE: Oh, Ed!

MARTIN: She's good fun.

CHLOE: Full of fun.

MARTIN: They're great fun.

SADIE: Oh, I can imagine.

ED: We wanted kids but it didn't happen.

A quick look passes between MARTIN *and* CHLOE.

SADIE: Never happened.

CHLOE: We don't try and we get pregnant. You do and it doesn't happen. Someone's playing a joke on us, aren't they?

SADIE: My very earliest memory is of seeing a little baby sitting on a picnic rug in the park. I must have been three or four. I was with my grandmother, feeding the ducks. I remember looking at this baby. I even remember that she was wearing a tiny little red velvet coat. You don't see babies in things like that these days. Maybe French babies. Imagine being a French baby! I mean, it's all downhill from there. Little red velvet coats. And I remember very clearly thinking: *I want to take it home.* We tried—

ED: We don't need to—

SADIE: No. The grisly details.

ED: We've let it go.

SADIE: Oh, indeedy. I'm not in therapy! Life doesn't 'owe'. It has no duty to offer things up.

CHLOE: Well—

ED: The world doesn't need to know—

SADIE: These days, it's all 'out there'. Every sordid secret—

ED: Don't know why we all feel every last thing has to be spilt—

SADIE: It's just—I feel as if… I don't know what's come over me. I feel as if I could talk all night.

ED: We like you.

Beat.

CHLOE: We like you too.

Beat.

ED: You're straight shooters. That's what it is.

MARTIN: Well, Ed, a little while ago we made a resolve, Chloe and I. We resolved that we'd be truthful.

CHLOE: Tell the truth. Come what may.

MARTIN: Chloe and I are both very aware of time. Of limited time. There are lots of things we want to do. Places we want to go. Experiences we want to have. We feel that we don't have time to waste.

CHLOE: We thought we'd conduct an experiment: we'd tell the truth and see what happened.

MARTIN: We know it's not always the smartest or kindest or most diplomatic or even the natural thing to do.

SADIE: Give us an example.

MARTIN: Well, I'm sitting here and I'm thinking… If I met you in another circumstance, I'd try to sleep with you.

Beat.

SADIE: Oh. [*Beat.*] Wow.

Beat. A tentative giggle, building. They are all laughing.

Oh, my Lord, Ed! Who are these crazy people?!

ED: I don't know, honey, but I like them!

SADIE: Oh, I like them, too. A lot more than Alison and Tony!

MARTIN: We promise not to bonsai!

CHLOE: What happens? *What happens?* we might ask ourselves. What happens if we only speak the truth to each other, if we create a friendship that's built on who we really are, not who we pretend to be or want to be, but *who we are*? The good and the bad. The great and the awkward. Because if we make that investment, surely … surely something great can come of that?

SADIE: [*moved*] Oh, bravo, Chloe!

CHLOE: Let's make a pledge tonight. Right here. The four of us. From this point on. We tell the truth.

MARTIN: To truth-telling!

They all raise their glasses and drink.

ED/SADIE/MARTIN/CHLOE: To truth-telling!

Beat.

CHLOE: We should seal it. You tell us something you've never spoken aloud before.

ED: What if there isn't anything?

CHLOE: Oh, Ed. Come, come.

SADIE: We're not interesting.

CHLOE: Of course you are.

SADIE: No, we're not.

CHLOE: Oh, you are so, Sadie.

SADIE: We're not!

CHLOE: You are, Sadie.

SADIE: We're not!

CHLOE: You are!

SADIE: We've never been interesting! *No-one showed us!*

CHLOE: Doesn't have to be scandalous. Just something that has not made it to the light. And then we'll drink some more and play some music until the sun comes up.

SADIE: You go first.

CHLOE: Alright, I will. [*Beat.*] When I was a kid we had a neighbour. An alcoholic divorcée. She was always calling my mother in and making her have a gin and listen to her sob stories. I couldn't stand the woman. I hated her lank, black pageboy with a blunt fringe and her awful mustard slacksuits. Her husband had left her because she couldn't have kids and taken up with a twenty-two-year-old waterskiing champion. I hated her face. She had these deep lines down the side of her nose and she sniffed all the time. Sinus. Anyway, one afternoon I was home alone—I was about twelve—and she came to the door and looked terrible. She'd clearly been sobbing. I said my mother was at the supermarket and she said to tell her she needed to see her right away. She said: *I'm desperate, Chloe. Do you know what that means?* My mother came home twenty minutes later and I thought to myself, if I tell her, she'll go over there and I thought: *Oh, let that stupid woman manage her own problems.* So I didn't tell my mother. And two days later, they found the neighbour's body. She'd hanged herself.

Beat.

ED: Still. Even if you'd passed on the message—

MARTIN: You never told me that story, Chlo.

CHLOE: You know, there's a tiny little bit of savagery in every single teenage girl. Teenage girls are perfectly capable of wishing someone dead because they don't like their hairdos.

ED: I didn't know that.

Long beat as they all take in the implications of this.

CHLOE: Sadie?

SADIE: Raincheck!

ED: Sadie doesn't have a story.

MARTIN: Come on, Sadie!

SADIE: Next time. I'll tell you next time.

CHLOE: What about you, Ed?

Beat.

ED: [*rising to the challenge, excited*] Alright. Okay.

MARTIN: Good for you, Ed.

ED: My mother. A story about my mother.

SADIE: Here we go.

ED: [*a sense that it's exceptional to hear* ED *speak this way*] When we visited my uncle one school holidays, she and my brother and I were picked up at the railway station. We were all getting into the car and there were only two safety belts and she raced to get hold of one, to strap herself in. I remember the way her fingers stretched, fast, over the green vinyl seat to secure that belt around her quickly. So we took the ride back to my uncle's, my brother unharnessed. She loved nothing and no-one, including my father to whom she was married for fifty-two years. She had no friends. She had no job. She had no interests. She didn't read. But that woman was seized up at the thought of death. Why? When being alive to her didn't mean love, the passionate longing for someone, the intense pleasure of the senses, the thrill of ambition, the tenderness of friendship, the wonder of life in all its odd encounters, its twists and turns—none of that. Being alive to her meant just that: physically having the blood circulate your body, the heart pump, nothing more, and yet she'd rather lose her child than her life. It was her, up against every other living thing. I've spent a lot of time thinking about that. Her hand grasping for the belt.

A long beat as they all take in the implications of this.

CHLOE: That's a sad story.

SADIE: Martin?

A deliberate sense of changing the mood.

MARTIN: Okay. I sat next to a woman on a plane and she asked me if I'd sleep with her.

CHLOE: Oh.

SADIE: Some women!

ED: [*relieved*] Only happened to me once, Martin. She was the four-hundred-pound captain of the Bulgarian hockey team! I told her it was against my religion to sleep with a socialist.

SADIE: He didn't want to hurt her feelings!

CHLOE: When *was* this?

MARTIN: A year ago.

CHLOE: A year ago?

MARTIN: When I went to Basel.

SADIE: And?

MARTIN: I said no.

Beat.

ED: That's it?

MARTIN: Yup.

SADIE: Oh, that's a cheat, Martin! That's such a cheat! It needs to be *a story*.

CHLOE: You never told me that.

MARTIN: That's the point, isn't it?

SADIE: Oh, come on, Martin. It's not a confession, it's a *story*.

MARTIN: Nothing happened.

SADIE: Make it up!

MARTIN: Make it up!

ED: Make it better.

CHLOE: Go on, Martin. Invent something.

MARTIN: Invent something?

SADIE: That's right! Make it interesting!

MARTIN: I don't know if I can—

SADIE: Of course you can!

ED: Just try!

CHLOE: Come on, Martin.

MARTIN: Okay… Okay, well… Uh… She was forty and she, ah… married a man she didn't love when she was nineteen.

ED: And?

MARTIN: [*gradually building*] And she'd never slept with anyone else and wanted to know what it felt like to have sex with another man.

SADIE: Well done!

ED: Keep going!

CHLOE: You're a creative guy.

MARTIN: [*building, until it is clearly from life*] She didn't love him but she respected him and she married him because he had the licensing deal for Coca-Cola in Croatia and was immensely wealthy and because he could whisper a poem in her ear and literally give her an orgasm without laying a finger on her. His father had died trying to pole vault over the Czechoslovakian border in 1968 and he'd grown up fatherless. She was on her way to a christening at a vineyard in Normandy. I made love to her in the shower cubicle of the Airport Westin Hotel Basel on my way to an art fair. She had a tattoo below her shinbone.

SADIE: Of?

MARTIN: A Vespa.

CHLOE: What poem?

MARTIN: [*quick as a flash*] Tennyson's 'Now Sleeps the Crimson Petal'.

A moment between them.

Light change. Shift. Beat.

To the audience:

SADIE: We all agreed to charter one of the hotel boats the following day. I think Ed was showing off a little, exaggerating his yachting abilities, but it was hot and sunny, perfect conditions for a sail. It was delightful—

ED: We saw dolphins.

SADIE: And a sea turtle.

ED: Chloe wore an orange bikini.

SADIE: She could certainly get away with it.

ED: No argument from me.

SADIE: It was a relief to be away from home. I felt as if—for the first time—anything was possible. Chloe and Martin weren't like our other friends. These people spent their days making tree houses out of bottle tops, or whatever! They thought *all the time*. About the world around them. About what things mean. And they liked us. They genuinely seemed to like us. Us! Ed and Sadie! Martin and Chloe—they were the future. They were the future and they looked at us and *we passed muster.*

ED: God, it was great not to talk about golf!

SADIE: We stopped mid-afternoon to eat in a pretty bay on the far side of the island. No-one there.

To each other:

MARTIN: What's art to you, Ed?

ED: To be honest, Martin, it's not a glass box.

SADIE: Oh, here we go. He can't resist.

CHLOE: Truth, remember?

ED: But if you tell me it's art, I'm prepared to accept that.

CHLOE: It's art.

ED: Okey-dokey.

MARTIN: Art.

ED: What is it?

MARTIN: Art is… life you can hang.

ED: Nicely put.

MARTIN: I admire you, Ed, for obvious reasons.

ED: And I admire you, Martin. I do. I'm caught up in the tiny little world of sales. A tiny little world. And you see the big picture for me, Martin. You see it for me, because I don't see it for myself. There are a million of me out there. And there's only one of you.

To the audience:

SADIE: And then the wind came up.

ED: The wind came up.

SADIE: How often do you hear that? The wind came up. Like: *He took a wrong turning*, or *She didn't give it a second thought*. You just know, you just hear those words.

ED: The wind came up and we agreed to head back. But in minutes, the sea had become quite choppy.

SADIE: Maybe we should remind everyone that you can't swim.

ED: I can't swim.

SADIE: Can't swim. Doesn't have a clue.

ED: Never learned to swim. My mother had a fear of water.

SADIE: Now, don't you always wonder when you read those stories about people near water who can't swim and then find they have to and drown, don't you always wonder: *Why? There are alps, aren't there?*

ED: I don't like to vacation in the cold. I make no apologies.

SADIE: I'll tell you why. Because they're arrogant.

ED: We were about a mile from the hotel jetty—just beyond seeing distance— It was lovely when we got the boat—

SADIE: A lovely, sunny day—perfect for boating—

ED: No-one was wearing life jackets. You may ask why not and you'd be right. But in our defence, it would have seemed utterly ridiculous when we took off. Because it was a millpond, a tourism ad. It was picture perfect.

SADIE: There we were, four perfectly normal white tourists in Prada sunglasses setting sail with a couple of bottles of Moët in the fridge and some club sandwiches supplied by the hotel kitchen.

ED: The resort staff set us up nicely, some basic instructions, but it was all very casual—

SADIE: We were very relaxed— Glorious bay, Michael Buble on the sound system. Absolute perfection.

ED: And then quite suddenly, the clouds came over and the wind came up—

SADIE: Quite suddenly. The wind comes out of nowhere. The sea starts turning—

ED: [*yelling to* MARTIN] *Wind's whipping up!*

MARTIN: [*yelling to* ED] Not too bad?!

ED: [*yelling*] What's that?!

MARTIN: [*yelling*] Not too bad. It's not too bad! We can tack!

ED: [*indicating the horizon*] I don't like the look of that!

MARTIN: See if it passes through! Five minutes!

SADIE: Looks nasty!

CHLOE: Is it okay?

MARTIN: It's a small front. I think we're okay!

ED: I don't like it, Martin!

MARTIN: Steady now!

ED: I'm going to swing her around!

CHLOE: I think I might be sick—

ED: Easy does it!

MARTIN: Grab the—!

SADIE: Careful of the—!

CHLOE: The boom, Ed!

ED *and* MARTIN *yell;* CHLOE *and* SADIE *scream: a cacophony.*

Then... silence.

He's under! My God!

SADIE: Oh, my God!

MARTIN: Jesus!

CHLOE: He's under! He's under!

SADIE: My God! My God!

CHLOE: He's gone under. Help! Help! Someone, help!

To the audience:

SADIE: No-one was on the wheel. It was pandemonium. I don't remember how I was feeling—it was as if my heart had gone cold, quite cold. Suddenly, Martin pulled off his shoes and then he threw himself in the water. Into the wild sea.

MARTIN *dives.*

CHLOE: [*screaming*] Martin!

Beat.

SADIE: And then it seemed as if Chloe and I were alone. Quite alone. It seemed like a long time. It seemed like hours. I thought: *Well, here I am at the beginning of a new life.* Just the grey waves and a sense of coldness taking hold of me. And then there was a noise and suddenly, Martin appeared, Ed in the crux of his arm and he was pulling him back towards the yacht and Chloe put the boathook over and somehow we leveraged Ed up, Chloe and I each taking one arm and dragging him over the rail and laying him out on the deck, and then Martin after him. Ed was unconscious. Well, more than unconscious.

ED *lies dead on the floor. An exhausted* MARTIN, SADIE *and* CHLOE *stand around him.*

He was dead.

MARTIN *starts frantically performing resuscitation.*

He had no pulse at all. I'd say for at least a minute.

CHLOE: [*distraught*] He's dead!

SADIE: He was definitely dead. [*Beat.*] I remember, very distinctly, saying to myself: *So this is where the story ends, the story of us.* Flirting on the twelve-fifteen. Dancing in the red dress. Seeing *The Blue Lagoon* at the Rockford Twin. Meeting under the clocks. The kiss at the waterfall in Vanuatu. The ring in the tiramisu. All of it. But Martin wouldn't give up. And then—

ED *coughs up sea water and 'comes to'.*

He came back.

SADIE: He died and he came back.

ED: The beach staff had seen us through binoculars and a speedboat came out to us and an ambulance met us at the jetty. We went to the local hospital for a few hours. They wanted to run some tests, but I persuaded Martin that the best thing would be to get home, see our personal doctors. Because, frankly, you just don't know.

SADIE: These places. I know it's patronising. It's cultural snobbery. They're probably fabulous doctors, fully-versed in natural therapies, mystical healing beetles, whatever. They might, in fact, know a lot more than us with our absurd obsession with science.

ED: But you just don't know.

SADIE: Well, you don't.

ED: And you're not going to test your liberal optimism in a situation like that, are you? You're going to revert to your natural position of Western scepticism.

SADIE: It's only sensible.

ED: Antibiotics and penicillin are our mystical healing beetles, aren't they? They're *our* cultural inheritance.

SADIE: Exactly.

ED: I was battered and bruised. Martin had dislocated his shoulder and broken a rib, but he was basically okay. The first flight out was at six a.m. We got back to the resort about three, had a rest and that night we all had dinner on our balcony. We were in shock.

SADIE: Some might say, surely, surely you wanted to be alone. After that. But I never wanted to be separate from Martin and Chloe again. I started shaking at the very thought of us leaving each other at the airport, going our separate ways. [*Beat.*] I had fallen in love.

SADIE: [*to* ED] What do you say?

ED: What can you say?

SADIE: You keep it simple.

ED: Yes, you do.

To each other:

[*To* MARTIN] You gave me back my life.

MARTIN: It's a new life, Ed. I hope it's a good one.

ED: I know you'll say that you just did what anyone would have done.

MARTIN: I don't know, Ed. I don't know that anyone would. But I did. I'm glad I did.

ED: Sadie and I—

CHLOE: Please, Ed—no big—

ED: I have to say—

SADIE: Let him, Chloe.

ED: We want to do something. We want to do something for you. Something that matters.

SADIE: Something big.

ED: Something that's going to mean something.

SADIE: [*to the audience*] Ed suggested we give them a horse.

CHLOE: A horse?

ED: It's just been born. Father was Whipitgood, mother's a lovely Irish mare. We can keep it for you and you can visit it. And it will make you a great deal of money.

MARTIN: I don't think so, Ed.

ED: This is a very promising horse, Martin. I wouldn't give you anything else.

MARTIN: Thanks, Ed, but no.

CHLOE: We couldn't. It's generous, but no.

MARTIN: The reward is that you made it, buddy. Listen to me, Ed. We went through something. We went through it together. That is the great gift we have shared. You don't owe us anything.

ED: That's beautiful, Martin, but I'm just a little bit more ordinary than you, remember? And I'm stubborn.

SADIE: He won't give up. I know this man. He's going to find something.

ED *gestures to* CHLOE *to dance to the music, which is getting louder.* CHLOE *starts slow-dancing with him.* MARTIN *starts to dance with* SADIE. *For a minute, all four of them are happily slow-dancing together in the semi-darkness. They stop.*

[*To the audience*] And then I had a bright idea. I said: *Let's meet again. In a year. To celebrate the first birthday of Ed's second life. And you two have to come up with something that we can do for you. A grand piano. A holiday in Portofino. A beach house. Anything.* And probably, just to shut us up, they agreed. And we swapped email addresses. And that, for the moment, was that.

They resume dancing. A few seconds. The lights fade to black.

END OF ACT ONE

ACT TWO

A year later. The sitting room of Ed and Sadie's very expensive, conservatively decorated city apartment. From a well set-up, easily accessible full bar, ED *is handing out French champagne.* SADIE, CHLOE *and* MARTIN *are all sitting. They all look just slightly different—different haircuts, et cetera. Indicating the subtle shifts of a year passing. The mood is 'up'.*

ED: I loved it.

MARTIN: You did?

ED: I loved it.

SADIE: We were so proud. I told the man standing next to me in the queue: *We're friends of the artist.*

CHLOE: That's sweet.

ED: Artists like you, Martin, they are… entrepreneurs of the soul.

MARTIN: [*touched*] Ed—

ED: You know the value of things. Things bigger than lathes and saws and sanders and edgebanders. I can't believe how narrow I used to be.

SADIE: Very narrow.

ED: Seeing things from such a cynical perspective.

SADIE: Very cynical. Always extremely cynical.

ED: Sadie, I'm managing to express myself quite well without any help.

SADIE: I'm affirming you, Ed. I'm supporting you fully in your self-condemnation.

ED: I went along without much hope, to be honest. It wasn't that I didn't trust you, Martin. I trust you profoundly. It's more that I didn't trust myself. I kept thinking of what you said about suspending doubt. I went and I walked around your glass box and I began to sense something, something about myself. That I couldn't be sure of who I was. There. That was the sensation. *Who am I?* I asked myself. The next day, Sadie suggested we go the Hayward Gallery. And the next day we went to the White Cube. The following weekend we were in New York and we went to the Guggenheim in Soho and a number of other galleries. There were things I liked and others I didn't. But what I realised was that each encounter had the possibility to… to surprise me about myself and the world. That sounds pretentious but the truth is, I began to get excited about what might happen.

MARTIN: I'm happy, Ed. I'm very happy. And touched.

ED: Life without enquiry… it's death. I went along and… I just opened myself to it. I banished doubt. I freed myself of doubt. And the moment you do that—it's like a jolt of electricity passes through you. I loved it, Martin. You've made me love art.

CHLOE: That's so moving, Ed.

ED: I feel privileged to count you as friend.

MARTIN: Likewise, Ed.

ED: No, but you're an exceptional person, Martin.

MARTIN: Oh, Ed! Steady!

ED: I see things as I see 'em. And I'm not an idiot.

MARTIN: You're a very smart guy.

ED: You're a genius.

MARTIN: Not so. But I'm glad you liked it, Ed. I'm touched you bothered.

ED: 'Bothered!' '*Bothered*'! It was our *honour*. It was our *privilege*. I never realised…

SADIE: It's been something of a revelation.

MARTIN: Never too late.

ED: All because of you two.

CHLOE: Not at all.

ED: If I hadn't met you…

MARTIN: You two would have discovered things without—

CHLOE: You have a tremendous 'life force'. You really do.

SADIE: No, it's about you two—

ED: Two gifts you've given me.

MARTIN: No, no, no.

ED: I realise now… Really great art—it's visual jazz, Martin.

SADIE: Now he wants a Martin Creed.

ED: He's done a very interesting piece at the Lehmann Maupin: a door that opens and closes.

CHLOE: [*surprised*] Oh, it's terrific.

ED: It's not derivative in the least. I don't know how Claringbold could have said that. You really have to wonder about the critics. Contemporary art is created in a context where the intellectual and political conditions make commentary about it completely dysfunctional.

MARTIN: [*very surprised*] Oh.

ED: I'd love to get my hands on a Creed.

CHLOE *glances quickly at* MARTIN *a moment.*

CHLOE: He's marvellous.

MARTIN: And a nice guy. We met him at Frieze. A tiny bit mad possibly, but awfully nice.

ED: I do like the ironic citing of the everyday in art.

MARTIN: U-huh.

ED: It's understandable that the question comes up: *Is it a wank?* But I think the studious exploitation of one's own daily life is completely justifiable. Art is personal. It has to be. And it always has been. The celebration of your own nerve endings, your own history, your own anger, your fear.

CHLOE: Gosh.

SADIE: See?

ED: There was a wonderful work in the Saatchi collection where you walk out over a pool of black oil. It's such a raw, pure, beautiful, exciting moment. A sea of glistening black surrounding you. You can go on and on about the existential claims of the unified form and so on, but it's really just about standing there in the gleaming darkness, contemplating diving in. A kid on a pier at night.

MARTIN: Ed… I'm— It's extraordinary.

SADIE: I told you. It's a new Ed. He's… younger.

CHLOE: Fantastic.

SADIE: He uses words like 'awesome'.

ED: We're so saturated in media, we're so informed, we don't invite information, it floods us. Every day is a deluge. Our imaginations are constantly—well, at war—with all those facts coming our way… It's so hard to be surprised by yourself. I've spent a year finding out about things. I realise that in my own way I was very snobbish. I was a snob. I thought I was too good for art.

Beat as MARTIN *and* CHLOE *take in* ED*'s transformation.*

Anyway… Happy anniversary!

SADIE/MARTIN/CHLOE: [*to each other*] Happy anniversary!

ED: Sadie's been cooking since February.

SADIE: I've gone Moroccan.

ED: Sadie's had her own little epiphany on the spice front. How's the hotel—?

CHLOE: Amazing. You really shouldn't—

ED: We checked it out on TripAdvisor—

SADIE: There were some plumbing issues, but apparently their algae wraps are to die for.

MARTIN: I love sushi—

SADIE: No, you get wrapped in algae. The day spa. Millions of undersea minerals plump your collagen levels or whatnot.

Laughter.

We have a full weekend. There are so many places to take you!

CHLOE: The apartment is lovely— It's a lovely apartment—

ED: We should drop the itinerary and just drink wine and play jazz.

SADIE: We love apartment living—

CHLOE: I can see why. The space—

ED: We can just close the door and walk away—

SADIE: I don't know how French provincial you are, but there's a delicious *armoire* I wanted to show you. Being a visual person, you could advise me.

CHLOE: Absolutely!

ED: It's a cupboard. A *cupboard*.

SADIE: It's a bit more than a *cupboard*, Edward Robert!

MARTIN: We're up for anything.

SADIE: I've been so looking forward to seeing you both.

CHLOE: It's great we could make this happen.

SADIE: We were determined. That's why we just emailed the tickets.

ED: No discussion will be entered into!

CHLOE: That was unnecessary.

SADIE: We weren't taking any chances.

CHLOE: Oh no. It was in our diary.

MARTIN: Wouldn't have missed it.

SADIE: We were so proud when we read about your inclusion—

ED: Todd Bunbridge-Hoffman came through.

MARTIN: I was a late addition, but apparently it was one of the most popular installations, so I was rather chuffed.

CHLOE: Bunbridge-Hoffman was thrilled. He loves Martin, as it turns out.

MARTIN: He's actually quite a nice guy. Not as intimidating as one might think. And not gay, interestingly.

CHLOE: We thought he was gay.

MARTIN: Proudly hetero as it happens and a bit of motorhead.

CHLOE: You couldn't believe the interest after that show opened. Martin's gallery was flooded with enquiries.

ED: Not surprising.

SADIE: That's marvellous.

MARTIN: A few really interesting commissions. A Mexican billionaire's become a bit of a fan. A gallery in Reykjavik.

CHLOE: We've had a really… a really significant year, actually. Sometimes nothing at all happens in a year. It's just a continuation. But these twelve months …well… you made us realise that we have to think again.

SADIE: Think again!

CHLOE: Rethink things. We've been suffering.

MARTIN: Yes, we have.

CHLOE: Inside certain beliefs. We build a prison. Couples do that: they build their own fortress, their confirm disaster for each other, they brick themselves in. We realised we had to get out of the fortress.

SADIE: I'm not sure I—

CHLOE: You were the key.

ED: That wasn't us, Chloe.

MARTIN: Actually, it was, Ed. That day on the yacht. Something started. Alright, perhaps it wasn't from us to you or you to us. But *between* us, between the four of us, something started.

CHLOE: Perhaps it was the summoning of a kind of… awareness. That time is precious. And that we all have to find a way of—

MARTIN: Overcoming obstacles—

CHLOE: Thinking differently, that's all.

MARTIN: Just like you, we started to get excited about what might happen.

CHLOE: We have to be brave.

MARTIN: That's it. I think we all feel that. That's what it comes down to. The boat. The year that's past. We know something that we didn't know in the same way before. *We just have to be brave.*

SADIE: I'm feeling brave! You two *make* me feel brave! Once upon a time I was sensible. But now I'm crazy! I'm crazy for anything!

ED: Lady Gaga, watch out!

CHLOE: We brought you a first birthday present, Ed.

SADIE: Isn't that sweet? How sweet.

MARTIN: [*bringing it out*] First pressing.

Beat as ED *takes it in: Miles Davis 'A Kind of Blue'. A penetrating moment.* ED *suddenly hugs* MARTIN, *then* CHLOE*—a real hug, full of longing and gratitude.*

Happy birthday to you.

ED *walks over to the record player and reverentially takes the record out of its sleeve and puts it on. For the first minute, he stands there.*

ED: You know, we can joke—

CHLOE: Believe me, he's not—

MARTIN: I'm not joking—

ED: I can tell you that whole thing has given me—

MARTIN: I know.

ED: It's something of a cliché, but—

CHLOE: We feel the same way. To come close to disaster—

SADIE: You're the same only—

CHLOE: Not quite.

SADIE: Not quite.

ED: We've stopped saying to ourselves: *We're* these *kind of people. We're the kind of people who drink pinot. We're the kind of people who vote this way.* We're not seeing ourselves as any kind of people anymore.

SADIE: We realised how we had settled into things—

ED: We found each other comforting. That's what we wanted. You choose comfort or you choose passion, and comfort seemed, somehow, more mature. Well—

SADIE: We've woken up to something—

ED: We're alive to something—the thrill of what might happen.

SADIE: One day he stayed home.

ED: We watched *Double Jeopardy* in bed in the middle of the day.

SADIE: He opened a bottle of Château Expensive. It was as if… as if our entire marriage had been one long cocktail party conversation. All the times we thought were… deep: the wedding, the conversations in the car coming home from dinner parties, the issues with health, the baby struggles, the sorrows… they'd all been chitchat compared with… We looked at each other—

ED: We did. You're the only ones we'd ever say this to.

SADIE: We saw inside each other with… complete clarity—

ED: With clarity and—

SADIE: And absolute courage—

ED: I felt like electric shock waves were going through me— It was awesome—

SADIE: We were both crying—

ED: I never cry—even with jazz—I'm not a crier. But the tears—

SADIE: Hello You, I said.

ED: Hello You—

SADIE: Said he.

Beat.

ED: I like my work. But it was also a refuge from the unknown. Since—well, I've begun to think—not that the unknown is less terrifying—

SADIE: It is terrifying—

ED: It *is* terrifying. But I've begun to think that in some ways, the terror—it's necessary.

SADIE: We're building an orphanage in Bali.

CHLOE: You and Ed?

SADIE: Not us. Not us, good Lord, I wouldn't know where to start. We're paying for it. And at some point in the future, we'd like to actually be a bit hands-on.

ED: We can make a difference.

SADIE: What a blessing that is for us. What a privilege that is. Lexus, orphanage, Lexus, orphanage: it's not rocket science, is it?

ED: Right now, we can help by writing a cheque. They know what they're doing. But at a certain point, we'd like to get our hands dirty.

SADIE: We're going to travel.

ED: I'm taking a sabbatical.

SADIE: We're going to go to New Guinea. No infinity pools. Just mosquito nets. And the odd headhunter. [*Beat.*] And it's all about that day.

MARTIN: We know.

SADIE: The moment life feels in jeopardy—

ED: Is the moment that wakes you up to life. People talk about dying and seeing the light, the tunnel, looking down. I don't know if there's anything in that or if it's all a lot of hokey-pokey and I don't care. But one thing I do know, is that you feel an adrenaline that's—

MARTIN: What?

ED: It's the excitement of not knowing what's going to happen next. Everything or nothing.

SADIE: I felt that too.

CHLOE: So did I.

MARTIN: Diving in, I had that feeling. Thinking, it could all be over or it might not.

ED: Exactly. Beneath the water, that's what I—that went through my mind—

MARTIN: And mine as I reached for you.

CHLOE: And mine on the deck.

SADIE: And mine, leaning over the rail and searching the waves.

ED: Something happened.

CHLOE: For us, too.

CHLOE *and* MARTIN *look at each other and smile.*

ED: I've never said this before. I can't even believe I'm saying it now. But it's as if you belong to us. And we to you. I just feel… I'm shocked that at my age, I could feel this way.

SADIE: It was as if you were sent.

Beat.

MARTIN: We're happy we were 'sent'.

Beat.

CHLOE: We feel as if *you* were sent to us.

Beat.

ED: I'm moved. I'm profoundly moved. I'm—

He starts crying. CHLOE *moves to him, wraps her arms around him. They embrace.* ED *keeps crying.* MARTIN *moves to* SADIE *and they embrace. The two couples hold each other tight, to the sounds of* ED *sobbing. Finally he stops. They pull back, reseat themselves. A moment of stillness and quiet.*

That's us.

SADIE: Now… the gift.

CHLOE: Oh!

ED: You promised.

MARTIN: We did.

SADIE: You promised us and we won't be dissuaded.

ED: You have to tell us.

SADIE: You promised. [*Beat.*] Say it. [*Beat.*] Chloe? [*Beat.*] Martin?

CHLOE: Alright.

MARTIN: Okay. If you mean it.

SADIE: You know we mean it.

ED: That's why we're here. Tell us and it's yours. If it's in our power, it's yours, Martin.

CHLOE: Well. [*Beat.*] We want you to listen.

MARTIN: Just listen. That's all. Just listen and then—

CHLOE: Then we'll see.

MARTIN: Okay?

SADIE: We'll listen.

ED: We're listening.

Beat. CHLOE *looks at* MARTIN.

CHLOE: How do we—?

MARTIN: I think I—

CHLOE: To begin?

MARTIN: Well. [*Beat.*] The customs dog—

CHLOE: Oh, Martin!

MARTIN: Why not? Why not start with the dog—?

CHLOE: Is that—?

MARTIN: It's a good place to start.

SADIE: The customs dog?

MARTIN: The little dogs that sniff your luggage—

CHLOE: I don't really think—

SADIE: The druggie dogs—

MARTIN: Exactly. The ones that are there in case you're, you know, the Prince of Darkness.

SADIE: They're so cute.

CHLOE: We wanted one. There was an ad.

MARTIN: You take one of those puppies and you have it for two years and then you give it back.

CHLOE: You train it. You fall in love with it. And then you give it back so it can sniff cocaine or… or… python eggs at airports.

MARTIN: You have to take it for walks in shopping centres and things. Get it used to people.

CHLOE: We got it. We called it Trey. A lovely little lab. But is this—?

MARTIN: We'll tell them about Trey and then we can—

CHLOE: But Martin—

MARTIN: We have to start somewhere.

CHLOE: That's not the right place to start.

ED: Can I just observe that you shouldn't give doggies gay names?

CHLOE: That's not a gay name!

ED: 'Trey'? It's got a yellow cashmere jumper thrown over its shoulders as we speak. Call it Rover and it has a fighting chance.

SADIE: I think Trey is a lovely name.

MARTIN: A great little pup. Wasn't he, Chloe?

CHLOE: We wanted to lavish things on it.

MARTIN: We bought it a lovely basket—

ED: Louis Fifteenth presumably.

CHLOE: A little tweedy rug with a bone in red blanket stitch.

MARTIN: Virginian ham. Lamb shanks.

CHLOE: We took it to shopping centres.

MARTIN: And we did love it.

CHLOE: He was so cute! Unbelievably cute!

MARTIN: Dogs lend an air of homeliness to things. I liked the connection I felt with the neighbourhood as I sauntered through it with Trey, smiling and nodding at the lady with the Doberman and the hairy man with the Jack Russells. It felt cosy knowing that we were fellow Dog People. I felt their benediction. They loved me. You went out into the world and you realised that all around you are the Dog People. And the Dog People are nice people. I felt at one with the Dog People.

CHLOE: Then we had to give him back. We'd been counting down the days, terrified.

MARTIN: She begged me to call them and offer to buy the dog. If we offered a colossal amount of money they might let us keep it.

CHLOE: But it was against policy. They wouldn't do it. Not for any price. He said: *Imagine if everyone did that? Blind people would be wandering through our community bumping into telegraph poles and the Princes of Darkness would use, unchecked, our transportation hubs for their own devious purposes.*

MARTIN: He had a point.

CHLOE: Of course he did.

ED: Trey probably wanted to go. Find a family that would call him Atlas.

SADIE: Shh!

MARTIN: The night before—
CHLOE: Inconsolable—
MARTIN: We patted him and held him.
CHLOE: We both cried.
MARTIN: It brought it all back to me. My childhood dog, Chutney.
ED: Chutney! Now it all makes sense.
MARTIN: A black lab. It all came flooding back.
CHLOE: We both had to have a Xanax. We were overwrought. He slept beside us.
MARTIN: I felt very low. I actually rang the Help Line, but when I said I was a conceptual artist, they hung up.
CHLOE: It was terrible.
MARTIN: Finally the day dawned and the lady came and collected him. We each gave him a pat. We wished him a good life. The lady took a final photo of us with him. She told us he looked well. And then we closed the door and Trey was gone.
CHLOE: He was gone. It was over.
MARTIN: We sat down and poured a drink.

Beat.

CHLOE: And then something strange happened.

Beat.

MARTIN: It came over us.
CHLOE: Something very unexpected.

Beat. ED *and* SADIE *are completely enthralled.*

MARTIN: Relief.
ED: Relief?
MARTIN: A weird kind of … liberation.
CHLOE: Almost euphoria.
MARTIN: *No dog.*
CHLOE: No dog. No dog food. No leads. No pooper scoops. No plastic bags. No squeaky toys…
MARTIN: I took the expensive, designer dog basket out to the footpath and put it there with a sign: ‘Free to a good home’.

CHLOE: We loved Trey, we did.

MARTIN: I believe we did love him.

CHLOE: But it's a wonderful feeling to be untied from that bind. It's a wonderful, free, light feeling. And we knew that we had the photos, to be looked at some point in the future and labelled 'The Trey Years', but that Trey was gone and we were over him.

ED: I see.

SADIE: Perhaps you didn't really love the dog?

MARTIN: No, we loved the dog.

SADIE: Maybe you *thought* you loved the dog—

MARTIN: I know we loved it, Sadie. I would have died for the dog.

CHLOE: The joy, the happiness, the lightness of being. We went out clubbing. We went out to a club and we danced and then we came home and we had sex on the stairs.

SADIE: Ouch.

MARTIN: That's the Trey story.

Beat. Silence.

ED: Okay, so. So how does this—?

SADIE: So what you want is—?

ED: I'm trying to find the connection here—?

SADIE: What is it that you want?

ED: You made a solemn vow—

SADIE: And we're not letting you go—

ED: We'll handcuff you, if we have to. You'll be force-fed couscous for months if necessary. You're not leaving until you tell us what you want.

MARTIN: Alright. Okay.

Over the next section, SADIE *and* ED*, very, very gradually begin to understand the proposition.*

CHLOE: The Trey story—

MARTIN: This story about Trey—

CHLOE: You see—

MARTIN: It got us thinking—

CHLOE: We couldn't help thinking—

MARTIN: Well, in the playground, in the park, another parent had a difficult child, a child that knocked our daughter over, a rough kid. And the mother apologised and made a kind of a joke. She said: *Alas! Too late to change my mind!* I laughed.

CHLOE: He laughed. There in the park. I laughed later, when he told me about it. And then—then we won the holiday.

MARTIN: That's right. That's what happened next.

CHLOE: We won the holiday and we met you.

MARTIN: We met you.

CHLOE: And everything that happened, happened.

MARTIN: And after everything happened, we went home.

CHLOE: We knew we were going to see you again.

MARTIN: We had a date, didn't we?

CHLOE: So you were in our minds. You weren't relegated to the past, to something that was over. You were the recent past and the near future.

MARTIN: And one night we were having a glass of red and we discovered that neither one of us had stopped thinking of that woman in the park who said it was too late. Too late to change her mind.

CHLOE: We talked about it. And then one night, we talked about Trey again. The Trey experience.

MARTIN: And somehow, that time with you… that time we spent… a few days plucked, somehow, out of ordinary life. Well, it got us—

CHLOE: Thinking. We were thinking. What if—?

MARTIN: What if the things that we've *done*—?

CHLOE: Which may not, in the bigger picture, have been the right things to do—

MARTIN: Maybe it's not impossible—

CHLOE: Perhaps it's not impossible to, in a sense, undo them.

Beat.

ED: Not following.

SADIE: I'm a bit lost.

Beat.

CHLOE: For quite a long time, I think we suffered in silence. I didn't want to burden Martin.

MARTIN: And I didn't want to burden Chloe.

CHLOE: I thought that perhaps if I stayed silent, those things that were wearing away at me might disappear.

MARTIN: But they didn't disappear.

CHLOE: Since we had Eleanor, something—something shifted—

MARTIN: We were excited—

CHLOE: We were excited by *life*!

SADIE: Children do that—that's what happens—

MARTIN: No, Sadie. No. *Before* Chloe got pregnant. *That's* when we were excited. I can't apologise for the fact that, back then, we were better people, because we felt great. People who are happy are nice. They're nicer. Happiness *makes* you nicer. It makes you generous. And both of us have felt that slipping away.

CHLOE: It sounds ordinary, but I had this book, this book I wanted to write—the thoughts wouldn't go away—

MARTIN: She's like me. We get obsessed with the thoughts in our head.

CHLOE: But every time I wanted to write, it was impossible.

MARTIN: A baby is top dog.

CHLOE: They have to be.

MARTIN: That's how they survive.

CHLOE: You literally can't ignore the cries.

MARTIN: And we started to fight.

CHLOE: We never fought. Not real fights.

MARTIN: I felt myself becoming ugly. As a man. I couldn't find any generosity.

CHLOE: I was worn out. There were days I wanted to… When I was a little girl, I used to walk home past a house that had a wild, rambling passionfruit vine, and in summer I would stop and pick a fruit and stick my thumb through the skin and suck in the juice. I longed for that. That moment again. Everything before me instead of behind. That would be a gift. Because I'd lost… I'd lost the will to love.

MARTIN: You lose the will to love each other.

CHLOE: You have to. Mother? Or wife? That's the choice.

MARTIN: No-one tells you. Beforehand. But the deal is: *your* love is second fiddle.

CHLOE: It dies. We could feel it dying. That's why—I mean—Martin's story about the woman on the plane—*Now Sleeps the Crimson Petal*—the shower cubicle—that's a story of approaching catastrophe. And Martin telling it, that night—the night of the stories— If that's not a sign—well. *Attention needs to be paid.*

MARTIN: One day we'd wake up and know that she and I—that we—that we had been subsumed.

CHLOE: That's how we felt.

MARTIN: So the mother who said to me that it was too late to change her mind made us wonder—

CHLOE: What if?

MARTIN: What if we *could* change our mind about the big things—?

CHLOE: What if those things weren't set in stone?

MARTIN: We had Eleanor.

CHLOE: We had her. It seems as if you have a child, there's no going back—

MARTIN: That's the accepted wisdom.

CHLOE: That's how people think.

MARTIN: But maybe—

CHLOE: This is what we were thinking. Maybe—

MARTIN: Perhaps it's not too late.

CHLOE: Perhaps it's *not* too late to change our mind.

A long beat.

ED: What?

Beat.

SADIE: What do you…? What does…?

ED: What?

Beat.

MARTIN: Perhaps the whole idea that these accidental acts become shackles—that fate knocks you to the ground and that there's nothing to do but accept it—perhaps—

CHLOE: Perhaps that's rather an old-fashioned notion.

MARTIN: These days we have a very strong sense of an individual's imperative. The imperative to be happy. Modern society is very articulate about the appropriateness of wanting or expecting personal happiness. But what if society condemns you, if it condemns you for trying to fix the thing that—that destroys you? Why can't we fix it? Wouldn't everyone be better off if we found a way?

CHLOE: That's what we thought. We thought that maybe we'd *all* be better off. Me. Martin. Eleanor.

MARTIN: What is right? What is right? What is *just*?

CHLOE: Maybe 'society' doesn't have a stranglehold on what is right. What if—in our case—we happen to know better?

Beat.

SADIE: Know better? [*Beat. Dawning*] You want us to… You want us to…?

Beat.

ED: You're joking.

Beat.

SADIE: You want us to—? [*Beat.*] Surely you don't—

ED: *You want us to… have Eleanor?*

SADIE: That's the gift?

Beat.

MARTIN: That is the gift.

CHLOE: The gift you want so much to give.

ED: What?

MARTIN: It would be the greatest gift, naturally.

ED: What?

SADIE: What are you saying?

CHLOE: Before you… I can see, Ed, that this is—that you can't quite—but listen. It's not what you think. I think it's not what you think.

ED: You want us to *have* your daughter?

SADIE: Eleanor?

ED: You want us to… You want to *give* Eleanor to us?

SADIE: What?

ED: What are you—?

SADIE: For a holiday? For a holiday?

CHLOE: Not for a holiday, no.

MARTIN: No, not for a holiday.

CHLOE: We're not bad people.

MARTIN: We're not.

ED: What is this?

CHLOE: I think you know that.

MARTIN: You do know that.

ED: What are you saying?

SADIE: I don't think we understand.

CHLOE: It's not because we don't love her that we ask you this.

SADIE: What?

ED: I'm at sea, I'm afraid.

MARTIN: Well—

CHLOE: No! You mustn't think that, Sadie.

MARTIN: No, you see—

CHLOE: We love her *too much.*

Beat.

SADIE: You love her too much?

CHLOE: Yes.

ED: You love her too much?

MARTIN: We love her too much to keep her.

Beat.

ED: Is this a joke?

MARTIN: No, Ed—no—

ED: Is this some kind of 'artistic statement'?

CHLOE: No!

ED: Is Todd Bunbridge-Hoffman going to burst through the door right now and declare this, this—this—request—declare it a work of genius?

CHLOE: No, Ed.

ED: Some peculiar piece of—of 'art'—that you have devised to—to be clever, to be cleverer than us, to take the mickey, to insult—
CHLOE: My God no, Ed! Not at all.
MARTIN: We would never do that. We have too much respect for you, Ed.

Beat.

ED: [*incredulous*] You want to give your child away?
CHLOE: Well—
SADIE: What?
ED: *Who does that?*
MARTIN: The thing is—
ED: What kind of a person does that? [*Beat.*] *Who are you*?
CHLOE: We're not good parents.
MARTIN: We're not very good.
SADIE: What?
MARTIN: We're not very good. Not at all. Despite all efforts.
CHLOE: It's true.
ED: You're not good parents?
SADIE: But that's crazy.
ED: You're crazy!
SADIE: That's crazy.
ED: You can't be serious.
SADIE: This is mad—
ED: You're insane.
MARTIN: We've tried—
CHLOE: We have. For five years we've tried—
MARTIN: We've tried and—
CHLOE: It's clear—
MARTIN: We have no talent for it.
SADIE: You have no talent for it?
CHLOE: We really don't.
ED: No talent?
MARTIN: No.
ED: No '*talent*'?

MARTIN: It's not a part-time—it's not—however much we like to think it's manageable—it's not a part-time occupation—

SADIE: Of course it isn't.

MARTIN: A child is not just for Christmas, as they say.

ED: What?

SADIE: But you're—you're *wonderful*. You two. My God. Yes. They're wonderful, aren't they, Ed?

ED: I thought they were.

SADIE: We said, we said to each other, that first night at the resort, we said: *They're wonderful.* Yes. *Kids,* we said, *kids these days… they're wonderful.* That's what we said. Didn't we, Ed?

ED: Yes.

SADIE: You're too hard on yourselves! You're way too hard on yourselves! My goodness, your standards are just much too high—

MARTIN: No, Sadie. Thank you, but—

SADIE: They're just too high, aren't they, Ed?

CHLOE: We're really no good. As parents, we're dreadful.

ED: Jesus! People have children. People do it. They don't *have* to be good at it! There's no benchmark. There's no standardised test. You do it because it's normal. You do it even if you're no good at it and eventually *they* will do it and try to be better than you. That's the way it's always been. It's not up to you—to *you*—

SADIE: Why would you say such a thing? Chloe? Chloe?

CHLOE: We don't know how to play.

ED: What?

SADIE: I'm sure you do. Everyone does.

CHLOE: Oh, no, Sadie. No. Playing is actually tremendously hard. We can't do it.

MARTIN: Our idea of a good time is… reading monographs on… on Bill Viola.

ED: Jesus.

MARTIN: We're hopeless at getting down on the floor.

CHLOE: We do it. Of course we do. But she knows we're terrible at it.

MARTIN: With the Duplo? Making houses? You tell a story together. With the little people? I start it, but then, I just lose interest. [*He holds up his hands as if he's holding little figures.*] She says: *Can I come over to your house, Billy?* And I say: *Sure Betty! Why don't you come over and we'll bake a cake!* And then she'll say: *I want to swim in your pool!* And I'll go: *What pool?* And Eleanor will say: *The pool! The pool!* And I'll say: *What pool?* And Eleanor will say: *That butter container is a pool, Daddy! Remember?* But I don't remember. She's made a world inside her head but it's not my world. I already have a world in my head and Billy and Betty don't belong there.

Beat.

ED: What the fuck?

CHLOE: She sees right through us. No-one tells you that basically, kids are smarter—

MARTIN: They are. They're smarter—

CHLOE: Smart kids are—

MARTIN: They're smarter than us.

CHLOE: She knows.

ED: My God!

CHLOE: She knows. She looks at us. And you can see her thinking: *These guys want something more.*

SADIE: What?

MARTIN: And if there's one irrefutable argument in this whole… picture… it's that a child is not fortunate to live with people who want other things… *more*.

Beat.

SADIE: What do you want more?

Beat.

CHLOE: Each other.

ED: Jesus!

ED *downs another drink.*

SADIE: Can't you have each other? *And* her?

CHLOE: We are… This is difficult to say… We feel as if…

MARTIN: There's no room. For anyone else.

ED: What?

SADIE: [*peacekeeping*] Just a minute, Ed. Just hold on a minute, Ed!

CHLOE: We've seen people like us… they are intent on preserving… But you can't. You have an emotional reservoir and when your children begin drinking from it, your husband drinks… *less*. It changes. The love moves into… it becomes organised around responsibility, around obligation and planning. It becomes a contract.

MARTIN: That's not—

CHLOE: We don't want a contract—

MARTIN: We believe in passion.

ED: What?

MARTIN: It shouldn't be wasted or diluted. You can't have everything.

ED: So—what? *She* goes?

MARTIN: It's us or it's her.

SADIE: But why… why would you choose 'you' over 'her'?

ED: This is unbelievable. This is—this is unbelievable. It's… unbelievable. You don't know how to *play*? You're completely off your rockers.

CHLOE: Ed, please. Please, Ed. Just hear us out.

SADIE: [*frightened*] Here them out, Ed.

ED: [*to* CHLOE] Is this… is this him? Is this him or is it you?

CHLOE: I always thought I wanted a child. I thought… I thought that's what a woman wants. But every waking moment is catapulted into sacrifice and inside me is a small, inextinguishable flame. It won't surrender to the forces of mothering no matter how hard I try to put it out.

ED: A flame? What flame?

CHLOE: I lie awake at night trying to extinguish it. But it will not die.

ED: Jesus.

CHLOE: I want to be good at this.

SADIE: Chloe—

CHLOE: I've longed to be good at this.

SADIE: Chloe, please—

CHLOE: You can't… you can't really evoke for anyone else…

SADIE: You don't have to—

CHLOE: [*breaking*] There's this guy… who, who parachutes from space to Earth. He freefalls—a thousand kilometres an hour—and that's how I feel. As if I'm freefalling in space. You say to yourself: *Be rational, this isn't rational, you're not being rational, try to be rational.* But another voice is louder. It's deafening. It says: *Go back!*

MARTIN *touches her tenderly.*

Some nights… I can barely breathe. There's a clique at school—

MARTIN: Spoilt brats—

CHLOE: They tell her they don't like her shoes—they say they're 'boy' shoes.

MARTIN: She comes home crying—

CHLOE: I lie awake at night wondering if I can call the other mothers. Do I call them? Do I tell them their children are going to grow up the kind of people who shoot people in public places? Do I tell them? Or do I rise above? Do I keep the social peace? Do I accept the lessons of the playground as a perfect precursor for life? And then there's the sheer logistics of another human being. The dentist and the doctor. The ballet classes and piano lessons. The pick-ups. The drop-offs. The social functions. I'm in the car for hours. Taking her to and from classes for things she has no real talent for, diligently affirming her self-delusions because apparently that's our job, the job of modern parents, to encourage our children to believe they are geniuses when they are quite, quite, irretrievably ordinary and will almost certainly become ordinary adults. Who picks up the pieces, Sadie?

SADIE: Who picks up the pieces?

CHLOE: When our children emerge into adulthood and find that, contrary to years of parental coaching, they are not, in fact, remotely special? What happens to those little hearts, nurtured on decades of white lies and narcissistic flattery? They explode in grief. They carry their sense of failure, of cataclysmic disappointment into marriages and parenting, into workplaces and love affairs. What kind of savage bequest is that? Is that *love*?

SADIE: I never thought of that. I suppose… I suppose that's true.

CHLOE: Don't judge me, Sadie. I need you.

SADIE: I need you too, Chloe.

CHLOE: Don't judge me yet.

SADIE: I'm listening.

CHLOE: You're an amazing woman, Sadie.

SADIE: I'm not amazing, Chloe. You're the clever one. Sometimes it seems to me that you're a bit too clever. It makes things complicated.

CHLOE: Sadie… you are amazing.

SADIE: I'm ordinary. I'm very ordinary. But I'm loyal.

CHLOE: Everything that makes Martin a great artist… it's at war with the father he might be. Everything that makes me a good writer… When we think of things, they're real to us. We imagine things for Eleanor and it's terrifying. It's unspeakable. We want to go to bed at night, to lay our heads on the pillow, and not feel unspeakable fear.

SADIE: Fear?

CHLOE: The way good things disintegrate: universities, rainforests, English curriculums, the Barrier Reef, handwritten correspondence. About the accidents that could befall…

MARTIN: The swine flu pandemics and the plane crashes, the careering cars, the bike wheels caught in tram tracks—

CHLOE: The tsunamis. I watched that footage over and over again, seeing us there, imagining her in my arms as the water surged— The paedophiles in European resorts, heroin, schizophrenia, the falling ladders, the planes in towers, ovarian cancer, the nuclear armaments, the financial crashes, chlamydia and cruel men. The children she will have who cause her pain. The men who will leave her. The employers who will sack her. The banks that will foreclose on her. The scars that will befall her. The unstoppable flood of disappointments.

MARTIN: This is love.

CHLOE: The children are born and the parents slowly, slowly, they die the lingering death of eternal hypotheses.

Beat.

SADIE: [*sweetly*] But—

CHLOE: What—?

SADIE: Well—

MARTIN: What—?

SADIE: Isn't that *how* you measure love?

CHLOE: What?

SADIE: By—by—the volume of—terror?

Beat.

CHLOE: I don't want to live in terror.

Beat.

MARTIN: It takes great care or great instinct. To grow a child. It takes one or the other. You have watch them. You have apply yourself.

ED: *So apply yourself.*

MARTIN: I can't do that. I can't watch. I can't apply myself. My mind is already…

ED: What?

MARTIN: I'm…

ED: What?

MARTIN: I'm… an artist.

ED: What?

MARTIN: I didn't ask to be. I didn't choose it.

ED: You're a father.

CHLOE: He's a father. Yes. But he's—he's—

ED: What?

CHLOE: He's an artist first.

ED: What?

SADIE: Now, hold on, Ed!

ED: You think—Jesus! You think you're *better* than other people?

MARTIN: My God, no! No, Ed. Of course we're not. If I could be… something that's *real*, that matters, that does something… a doctor or an irrigation specialist or an aeronautical engineer… I'd take that any day over, over— I would. I dream about waking up in the morning knowing with certainty that the day will accomplish something. That it will help to build a rocket, or find a cure or bring water to the desert… to know that. But I do something else. I dream. I dream for you, Ed. It's something I can do.

ED: Dream?

MARTIN: [*genuine*] Let me say it, Ed. Let me say what more people should say: My daughter needs someone better than me. I'm not a good father. I can't *make* myself be one.

ED: Other men do.

MARTIN: Other men… might try. Some may be. Of course. You. You for instance. You would be a good father, Ed.

SADIE: He's right, Ed.

ED: But I'm not a father!

MARTIN: I'm an artist first, Ed.

ED: An artist!

MARTIN: I'm an artist first. Even if I'm a bad artist.

SADIE: You're a great artist. Of course you are.

CHLOE: He has something—

SADIE: Of course he does—

CHLOE: It burns bright—

SADIE: It's important, Ed— It's— You *know* it is—

ED: 'It burns bright'? Are you all insane? What burns bright? A light that switches on and off, a door that opens and closes? An exploding room? A stuffed shark? A box? What planet are you from? *No-one's* an artist first!

CHLOE: Martin is at the top of his game. And in a way, I am too. When I write, it's incredible how the words move through me. They're the right words. It's something I can do better than other people. And Martin. Well, he's a genius.

SADIE: Of course he is. I'm quite sure Martin is a genius. Only—

CHLOE: Well?

SADIE: I think what Ed is saying is… Does it matter?

CHLOE: What?

SADIE: [*gently, not point scoring*] Does it matter? Really? I mean… Do we *need* another genius?

CHLOE: Sadie… I—I'm sorry, but—he can't let that go. Letting go of that… it's death.

Beat.

ED: Jesus H. Christ.

MARTIN: Ed, hear me out.

ED: There's nothing you can—

SADIE: Listen to him, Ed—

ED: [*to* SADIE] What's the matter with you?

SADIE: [*anger driven by fear*] Nothing! There's nothing the matter with me! Maybe there's something wrong with you!

ED: What?

SADIE: Maybe there's something wrong with you!

ED: What are you talking about?

SADIE: It never occurs to you. It's always the *other* person.

ED: What's gotten into you?

SADIE: You're not perfect.

ED: Who said I was perfect?

SADIE: We're all living in glass houses, that's the whole point.

ED: What? Everyone's gone mad.

MARTIN: Hear me out, Ed.

SADIE: Listen to him, Ed. They're sitting in our apartment, Ed. They're our *friends*.

MARTIN: You're a straightforward guy.

ED: Yes I am.

MARTIN: You say things—you talk—you talk straight.

ED: Yes, I do.

MARTIN: Guy to guy— It's not easy for a man to say: *I can't do this.* There are things we can't do, of course there are. But to admit it—

ED: Yes.

MARTIN: That's tough.

ED: I know—

MARTIN: It's tough to announce: I failed.

ED: Alright.

MARTIN: When I met you—I thought— *Okay, I'll be straight with you.* I thought: *This guy's getting on. He's got some dough. He's made a success of himself.* Not like my friends—all of us hungry for—for something—still clumsy in how we— No, I said: *Here's a guy who has climbed a mountain. He's at the top of the mountain. He knows a thing or two.* And I admired that. I liked you. I felt a strong sense that here was a man I could talk straight to, who could *listen*. A man to whom I could say: *I can't do this.*

ED: Well, I appreciate that, Martin. I do. But the fact is—I don't like it.

SADIE: Oh, my God!

MARTIN: You don't like it?

ED: No. I don't like hearing a man say: *I can't do this.* I don't need—

MARTIN: You don't?

ED: No. The truth. Don't need it. I'm happier to be deluded.

SADIE: Oh, for God's sake.

ED: It happens when you turn fifty. Faced with the unpleasant truth or a pleasant illusion, you take the latter.

SADIE: No, Ed! Remember?

ED: You take delusion. With gratitude.

SADIE: No, Ed! No!

ED: You want things nice.

SADIE: This year, Ed—

ED: No, Sadie—

SADIE: It's been an incredible year, Ed. For us—

ED: But Sadie—

SADIE: Things changed. They changed for the better.

ED: What do you want, Sadie? You want me to *pretend*—?

SADIE: Since we met them—since the accident—you found something, Ed! *We* found something. Don't—

ED: Sadie— Do you—? Really?

SADIE: I'm not taking sides, Ed. I'm giving them the benefit. I'm not taking sides. I'm not against you, Ed. I promise. I'd never be against you!

ED: What's gotten into you?

SADIE: They're not like us.

ED: No, they're not.

SADIE: That's *why* we like them.

ED: Do we? Do we, Sadie?

SADIE: [*in desperation*] I'm just saying, Ed… I'm just saying… *Don't. Go. Back.*

Beat.

MARTIN: I'm not comparing myself to—to— But, Ed, where would we be if artists stilled every unusual thought? What if every passion was quelled because it seemed… too badly behaved? What if artists said no to the part of themselves that singled them out? What would we have, Ed? We wouldn't have *The Marriage of Figaro* or *Anna Karenina*. We wouldn't have Van Gogh's starry nights.

ED: What?

MARTIN: Don't you think—?

ED: [*disbelieving*] *What*?

MARTIN: Don't you think there's a price worth paying?

Beat.

ED: A price?

Beat.

MARTIN: The price we pay to be an interesting civilisation is tolerating the uncivilised.

SADIE: There's room for us *and* them!

Beat.

CHLOE: That night at the resort. We all felt it.

SADIE: We felt—?

CHLOE: We—we—fell in love. Didn't we?

ED: I don't know about *that*—

SADIE: Of course we did. We felt it too.

MARTIN: I think we fell. I think we four—we fell—

SADIE: I think we did. Yes, we did.

MARTIN: But it wasn't until afterwards, when we were home—

CHLOE: It just hit us. *You're the ones*.

ED: Is that what you're going to tell her, Chloe? You're going to say: *We met these people on vacation. We gave you to them.*

CHLOE: At first… just a long weekend.

ED: Right.

MARTIN: Then—well then, maybe, a couple of weeks.

CHLOE: [*thinking in the moment*] We'd say that we're travelling in—in Europe, you know, for Martin's work. Six months or so. And then at the end of the six months, we revise it.

ED: Oh, you would?

MARTIN: And if you had grown to feel something for Eleanor—

ED: Like a little puppy—

MARTIN: If you loved her, we'd—we'd just… keep going.

ED: My God. [*Beat. Quietly*] My God… Jesus… Pass me a bottle.

SADIE *moves to pass him the bottle of wine.*

No, no, *the Scotch.*

She passes the Scotch and, as the conversation continues, he pours and downs a large slug. SADIE *follows.*

MARTIN: We love our daughter.

CHLOE: We adore her.

MARTIN: She's a wonderful child.

CHLOE: She's a beautiful little girl.

MARTIN: We're happy we had her. We're glad she exists. We want her to have a wonderful life.

CHLOE: The best life. A true life.

MARTIN: We want the very best.

CHLOE: And you *are* the very best.

MARTIN: And you can give her a wonderful life.

SADIE: Us?

CHLOE: Yes, Sadie. You're two wonderful people.

ED: What? No—I—

MARTIN: No, Ed. It's true. You're intelligent and kind. You believe in important things. You like children. You *wanted* children. And we have a child who, frankly, would be better off with you.

ED: You think so?

MARTIN: We've wrestled with it—with all of it—and one thing we know with certainty is—

CHLOE: You'd be better than us.

ED: Maybe you're right.

MARTIN: You two have a gift. A gift for giving. Which we don't have. You are what every child should have.

CHLOE: We look at you two and we see good people. Good people. People whose first calling is to do the right thing.

MARTIN: The right thing. The decent thing.

CHLOE: Forgive me if I'm wrong—if we've misjudged—but you two don't need to—to make your mark—

SADIE: I'm not making any marks. I'm just not into mark-making.

MARTIN: [*to* ED] You've made your mark—

CHLOE: You don't feel that—that need to put yourself—at the centre of things.

MARTIN: You'll put *her* at the centre. I know that.

CHLOE: We can't do that. There's something about us that just—can't let go of our own—

MARTIN: Potential.

ED *stands up.*

ED: [*with growing passion, certainty*] I know that you're artists. You're artists and you live a different way, you answer a different calling. I'm not saying that you shouldn't be whatever… you shouldn't do things differently. But I don't think we should just go around saying things like it is. Okay? Okay? If that makes me a bore, so be it. We make mistakes, of course we do. We make choices and they're the wrong choices. We fall into things and they're… wrong for us. *But we see it through.*

MARTIN: With respect, Ed, I don't think you're thinking clearly—

ED: 'With respect'! Why don't you shut the fuck up?

SADIE: [*sarcastic*] Fantastic!

MARTIN: I think, if you're reasonable—

ED: I think you should go.

SADIE: [*frightened*] Oh, Ed, don't be ridiculous! We can be—

ED: No.

SADIE: Civilised. For God's sake! We—

ED: No. I want you to leave!

SADIE: They can't leave!

MARTIN: Ed—this is the man who said to me, tonight, when we arrived how excited he'd become 'about what might happen'. 'Life without enquiry… it's death,' you said. And you were right. You became excited about what might happen and this has happened. *This. Us. We* have happened to *you.*

SADIE: This is Martin and Chloe, Ed.

MARTIN: It's us, Ed. And it's okay—

ED: No. Why don't you just shut the fuck up like a good little genius?

SADIE: But Ed—

ED: *No!* [*Beat. Upset*] This is no way to— This is no way to— Some things should never be said.

MARTIN: I don't believe that, Ed. I don't believe that you believe that.

ED: You give space to those thoughts and they'll overtake—they'll swallow up the part of us that does the right thing. Because it's the right thing. Not because it's instinct or what we want. But because it's right. And if something natural gets lost in that, well—*good.* That's a good thing. Natural isn't best. We've had millions of years to comprehend that our instincts aren't the basis for a healthy way of life. We have to sit on our instincts quite a lot of the time to make things work. And that's okay. It's better than okay. It's *necessary.*

SADIE: Ed—

MARTIN: For God's sake!

> ED *swings around and hits* MARTIN *in the face. The women leap up as the blow lands.* SADIE *and* CHLOE *start yelling.* MARTIN *reels, falls back, lands across a chair. His nose is bleeding.* SADIE *goes to* MARTIN*'s aid.* MARTIN, SADIE *and* CHLOE *are still talking, helping, gathering themselves. As the women help* MARTIN *onto his chair,* ED *turns away casually, walks over to his glass and has a drink. Silence. Beat.*

[*Nursing his wounds*] I love that little girl. [*Beat. With real pain, growing desperation*] I love her. I look at her sleeping. I tuck her in. There's nothing ruined there. I look at her, at that sleeping child, and I have this sense of awe, this awe that there lies a human being completely… *pre-ruin*. There's nothing damaged or besmirched or disappointed. I look at her and I think to myself: *Can I honour that? Can I be the one who leads her, leads her out into the… the full, cold glare of life?* I can see your arms around her. I look at her and I can see you there. Holding her. Whispering stories to her. Leading her on her first pony. Attending parent-teacher interviews and caring. Walking down the aisle with her. My little girl.

ED: Don't say it, Martin. I don't want to hear it!

MARTIN: The morning she was born, Chloe and I, we—felt —invincible. Hello, we said to her. Welcome to the human race. I left Chloe in the evening and went home. It was a freezing night and the house felt like a crypt. I lay in bed and thought of Eleanor in her plastic bassinette and Chloe beside her. I thought: *What have we done?*

The sadness of this registers in ED.

We'd do anything to save her.

Beat as they absorb this.

SADIE: You think they should 'see it through'? What does that mean, Ed? 'See it through'. And all those years ago, you and I, we sat on a doorstep in winter and I said to you: *It's happened.*

ED: No.

SADIE: I said: *It's happened and now what?* You were twenty-one years old. I was nineteen years old. And you and I, we said: *This will ruin our lives.*

ED: We were young.

SADIE: We were young.

ED: We had plans.

SADIE: Yes, we did.

ED: It wouldn't have worked.

SADIE: Well, who knows? Who knows?

ED: We didn't know what we were doing. We were children ourselves.

SADIE: Twenty-year-olds have babies and somehow the babies grow into children and then into adults. The parents grow into middle age and old age. The clock keeps ticking. The hearts keep beating. Life goes on. We could have had the child but we chose not to.

ED: Sadie—

SADIE: We made a decision, Ed. We might have seen ourselves another way. Our own lifespan gaining eighty years and another after that as our own genes unfolded before us. Stretching out forever and taking with them your blue-green eyes, your neatness obsession, your aversion to capers…

ED: Please, Sadie—

SADIE: But we made a decision, Ed. And I know there have been times when we've looked at each other and thought: What is it here that's worth saving? What a shock that is to find… that on some level you need love to *have a point*.

Beat.

ED: What do you want? You want me to say: *Guilty! I'm guilty!* And give them leave to renounce—to *renounce*—

SADIE: I want you to… suspend doubt.

Beat.

ED: You want to—? Sadie?

SADIE: I admit this is all a little crazy. It's a bit… disturbing.

ED: It's 'a bit disturbing'.

SADIE: We were thinking about Rolex watches or a holiday in Belize. But Chloe and Martin are our friends. And just by the by, *they saved your life*. So I think that maybe we can find a way to accept what they're saying is said in… in good faith.

ED: Faith in what?

SADIE: Well. Faith in friendship. Friendship should withstand certain… aberrations. It should be stoic in the face of… eccentricities.

CHLOE: I knew you'd be able to see—

MARTIN: She had faith—

SADIE: [*flattered*] Well—

MARTIN: She said to me: *She'll get it*—

SADIE: Oh well—

CHLOE: *Wouldn't the world be a better place if children belonged to those who wanted to be belonged to?*

SADIE: We might not like it but there is—there is some sense in that.

ED: Sense?

SADIE: Well, isn't there?

ED: What's wrong with them? What's wrong with these people? [*Looking at them*] What's wrong with you?

SADIE: We took them on.

ED: What?

SADIE: We took them on. We took them on.

ED: Sadie—

SADIE: That means something, Ed. They belong to us now. And we belong to them. Get off that high horse for just a second and think this through. If you send Martin and Chloe away now, *we're never going to see them again*. They'll be gone. They'll seem like—like a figment. And we will lose—we'll lose. It's not just them we'll lose, Ed. Is it? Is it, Ed? We'll say—we'll say: *They came and they went. They left us. They left us all alone*. Is that really what you want?

ED: [*softly*] But Sadie. This is… this is not our business.

SADIE: They've— Ed—! They've *made* it our business. It *is* our business. Because they're here. It's said. They've said what they've said. They said it out loud and we heard it. We heard it, Ed. So it *is* our business!

ED: We were thinking of giving them a horse, Sadie—

SADIE: I know that, Ed—

ED: A *horse*—

SADIE: Yes—

ED: Giving *them* a horse, not—

SADIE: I know—

Beat.

CHLOE: At the resort… you said, remember? You said that you were looking to find something… something that was missing…

SADIE: We were. Weren't we, Ed?

ED: That's nothing to do with it.

CHLOE: We felt it. Martin and I. We felt it.

MARTIN: We went to bed and we said to each other: *These are good people. These people love each other. But there's something—there's an absence—there's a vacancy—*

SADIE: That's what it is—

CHLOE: And that vacancy is not going to be filled by a resort holiday.

MARTIN: We felt it even without knowing you. We watched you the day before. We watched you at the pool. *Something is missing.*

CHLOE: Something is missing. We felt it.

MARTIN: Two people who, for whatever reason, are *minus something.*

Beat.

ED: [*to* SADIE] What do you want from me?

SADIE: What?

ED: What do you want? What do you want from me?

SADIE: I want— [*Beat. She looks at him tenderly.*] Didn't we always—?

ED: Oh no!

SADIE: Come on, Ed. Didn't we—?

ED: No, no.

SADIE: We knew. We know. We've always known.

ED: No.

SADIE: Ed, whatever you might think. Whatever you might—whatever is going on in there—*we always meant to be three.*

A long beat. Something has softened in ED.

MARTIN: I'm hungry.

ED: You're hungry?

MARTIN: Why don't we eat?

ED: We're not eating! No-one's eating around here!

CHLOE: We could eat. We could all calm down. We could let it sit.

SADIE: There's a lot of food. I've got a kitchen full of tagine.

ED: As if things weren't bad enough.

MARTIN: We should eat. I'm hungry.

SADIE: I'm going to tell you my story. And then we'll eat.

ED: You don't have a story.

SADIE: Yes I do. I do have a story. Everyone else told a story. I want to tell mine.

ED: What story?

CHLOE: Tell your story, Sadie.

ED: Tell your story, then.

SADIE: And then?

ED: Tell it.

SADIE: When I was five years old, we used to visit my Aunt Helen every Sunday. We had to take a ferry there. From Circular Quay, across the harbour. And every Sunday we'd get nicely dressed and my mother would take me and my sister Lil to buy the ferry ticket and then while we waited for the ferry, she'd buy us an ice-cream cone.

ED: Sadie, is this—?

SADIE: I was eating my ice-cream when then this kid, this boy, about my age, about six, stared at me and made a face.

ED: Ah, Sadie—

CHLOE: Let her speak, Ed.

SADIE: Whenever my mother turned around he smiled at me and whenever she turned away he made a disgusting face at me. I can still remember his awful face. Nasty, scrawny little kid.

ED: [*helping himself*] Time for another drink, I think.

As SADIE *tells her story,* CHLOE *and* MARTIN *give her their full attention.* ED *begins by blithely serving himself a drink, not paying attention to* SADIE*, even actively distracting. But as the story continues, he begins to turn his attention to what* SADIE *is saying until, by the end, he is entirely captivated by it.*

SADIE: So the ferry comes in and we get on and he gets on, too, with his parents. And the ferry leaves and the water's choppy, but I'm used to it, I make the crossing every Sunday. Sometimes I go and talk to the crew or go out to the bow and look out over it across the harbour. Sometimes I whistle a little tune, a little sea shanty my father taught me. *What shall we do with the drunken sailor? What shall we do with the drunken sailor?…* So I go wandering off, I'm making my way towards the side of the ferry and this kid, he keeps following me. My mother and sister are in the cabin and so are his parents. So I move across to the other side of the boat and he follows me, all the time making these faces at me. He comes up to the side, where I'm standing. And he says something very unpleasant. And I tell him to shut up. And he says it again. And I say: *Don't say that.* And he says it again and so I push him off.

Silence.

ED: What?

SADIE *turns her full attention to* ED. *There is an element of absolute provocation directed at him.*

SADIE: I gave him a shove.
MARTIN: You—?
SADIE: And over he went.
ED: What the—? You threw a kid overboard?
SADIE: I pushed him and he fell.

A stunned silence. ED *is completely crushed by this story. A long beat.*

And now, Ed?

He's still pulling himself together.

MARTIN: Tell us to go and we'll go.

CHLOE *stands up, picks up her bag, her coat.*

SADIE: *No-one's going anywhere.*
ED: Everyone's said their piece, haven't they?
CHLOE: I know I have.
SADIE: We all have.

Beat. ED *weighing. He and* SADIE *look at each other.*

ED: [*to* CHLOE, *quiet, defeated*] Sit down.
SADIE: [*bolstered, happy again, in more control than she's ever been*] Sit down, Chloe. Sit down, honey. Let's all sit down. We'll drink some wine. In a minute, I'll get the food. We'll eat the couscous. It will be fragrant and delicious. We'll feel better with some food.

[*Beat.*] There's nothing to do but go forward. Like friends do. Like real friends do.

Very gradually, the lights come down over the following section. CHLOE *sits.* SADIE *and* ED *become increasingly involved in what they are hearing, drawing near. All four become a huddle.*

At the same time, in a corner of the stage, the lights come up on a glass box. Inside the illuminated box is a little girl, around four. None of the four notice her.

MARTIN: She's very neat. She keeps her things tidy. She makes little piles of things.

CHLOE: She makes lists. If she doesn't know how to write the word, she draws it. Lists of her favourite things. Lists of the books she likes. She finds structure liberating.

MARTIN: She likes shoes.

CHLOE: If she's upset, just take out your shoeboxes.

MARTIN: High heels. Things with sparkles she especially loves.

CHLOE: She loves sparkles.

MARTIN: Last year every meal had to be white.

SADIE: White?

CHLOE: The food had to be white. Rice, bread, chicken fillets, yoghurt. If it wasn't white, she wouldn't eat it. Don't worry, she's grown out of it and it's perfectly normal.

MARTIN: When you're four, you're almost completely obsessive-compulsive, but on your fifth birthday, it goes.

CHLOE: Ask any paediatrician.

MARTIN: It's actually *good* to be strange when you're four.

CHLOE: She loves the water. She's very confident in the water. A little fish.

MARTIN: She sings.

CHLOE: She has a lovely voice and she sings lullabies in Spanish. Beautiful lullabies.

MARTIN: She's terribly sweet the way she sits there and just starts singing.

CHLOE: [*singing with the hand gestures of a little bird*] 'Pio… Pio… Pio…'

MARTIN: She likes to fall asleep to the sound of someone reading to her.

CHLOE: You can't finish the book, you just read on and at first she closes her eyes—

The lights come down as they are continuing to speak.

MARTIN: But she's listening. You can't stop or she'll be cross with you.

CHLOE: And then you see her chest rising and falling, that steady rise and fall and you know…

THE END

www.currency.com.au

Visit Currency Press' website now to:

- Buy your books online
- Browse through our full list of titles, from plays to screenplays, books on theatre, film and music, and more
- Choose a play for your school or amateur performance group by cast size and gender
- Obtain information about performance rights
- Find out about theatre productions and other performing arts news across Australia
- For students, read our study guides
- For teachers, access syllabus and other relevant information
- Sign up for our email newsletter

The performing arts publisher